'I cannot imagine a better treatment on a more timely subject. Liam touches the very heart of the gospel. Every Christian should read this book. It is old-fashioned reformed theology with a contemporary flair.'

R.T. Kendall

'This outstanding book walks straight out of the text of Colossians 1 verse 28: "We proclaim him, admonishing and teaching everyone with all wisdom." Liam Goligher proclaims the theme of the Lamb of God and gives the reader a unique Bible overview, whilst at the same time admonishing the false teaching in the church and the culture, which seeks to undermine this central Bible truth. Liam Goligher has done a remarkable job in serving the church with this book.'

Rico Tice, All Souls, Langham Place

'This magnificent sweep through the story of redemption leaves absolutely no place for some of the recent, but as Liam points out truly not so recent, ideas troubling the evangelical church at this time.'

Peter Maiden

'You hold in your hands a book that both warns of recent redefinitions of the Christian faith and defends the gospel – the only message that can prepare us for eternity. This book is a solid reminder that all attempts to dilute the gospel empty it of its power and wonder.'

Dr. Erwin Lutzer, The Moody Church

'This book sweeps us through God's plan of redemption, from before creation to the new creation. Liam Goligher has got to grips with the atonement as it is revealed in the Bible, a strong thread woven through Scripture. If you want the biblical teaching on redemption – this is it . . . Intelligent, well-written and passionate.'

Stephen Gaukroger

'Liam Goligher, one of the UK's finest Bible teachers, warmly, thoroughly and convincingly explains what the Bible teaches about Jesus' death on the cross. This is spiritual food at its best, dealing with the heart of the Bible message and the Christian gospel itself. I urge you to read it!'

Roger Carswell, author and evangelist

'I am delighted to commend this apologetic of the traditional theological understanding of Christ's work on the cross. At a time in which the debate about the passion has become so prominent, it is crucial that evangelical Christians understand the biblical exegesis of what Jesus did.'

Rob Frost, Share Jesus International

'It has become almost virtuous amongst some evangelicals to be uncertain about things once certain, confused about things once clear and sentimental about things once serious. If the church is to be always contemporary, it must deal with truths that are eternal. This book reaffirms the vibrant, eternal truths of the gospel that are being neglected by some and denied by others.'

Charles Price, The Peoples Church, Toronto

'Confused about terms like "the wrath of God", "penal substitution", or "cosmic child abuse"? Not sure precisely why Jesus died and what it has to do with practical Christian living today? If so, *The Jesus Gospel* is for you. Allow it to clarify, illuminate and inspire you afresh for Christ and Him crucified.'

Steve Brady, Moorlands College

'Dr Liam Goligher's enviable gifts as a communicator and his astute theological mind here combine in his new book, *The Jesus Gospel*. Its exposition of the Bible's basic plot-line help us to answer a fundamental question on which Christians today are often confused – *What is the Gospel of Jesus?*'

Sinclair B Ferguson, Westminster Theological Seminary

'Accurate, wide-ranging canonical exposition of Scripture at a non-technical level here displays salvation through penal substitutionary atonement as central to the message of the Bible as a whole and to Christ's own understanding of his Father's plan. Goligher covers this familiar ground in a gloriously head-clearing, heart-warming way.'

J.I. Packer, Professor of Theology, Regent College

'Bible doctrine doesn't need to be re-invented for each new generation, it simply needs to be re-discovered. The best interpreters act like tour-guides who've lived in the area for a long time, know the language and local history, and can reveal surprises usually missed by day-trippers in a hurry. Liam Goligher is one such guide. He traces the blood-stained path of God's rescue plan for mankind, casting fresh light on familiar biblical events and making the Cross stand out so ruggedly that you could splinter your finger on it.'

Greg Haslam, Westminster Chapel

'Liam has written a bold and beautiful book which astutely clarifies our thinking about Jesus and his mission. Read it and be prepared to be newly excited about the awesome work of the Cross.'

John Benton, Editor, Evangelicals Now

'A new and fresh treatment of an essential doctrine.'

Robert Amess, pastor, speaker and writer

The Jesus Gospel

Liam Goligher

Authentic

12 11 10 09 08 07 06   7 6 5 4 3 2 1

First published 2006 Authentic Media
9 Holdom Avenue, Bletchley, Milton Keynes, Bucks,
MK1 1QR, UK
and 129 Mobilization Drive, Waynesboro, GA 30830-4575, USA
www.authenticmedia.co.uk
Authentic Media is a division of Send the Light Ltd., a company
limited by guarantee (registered charity no. 270162)

British Library Cataloguing in Publication Data

A catalogue record for this book is available from the
British Library

ISBN-13 978-1-85078-698-6
ISBN-10 1-85078-698-4

Cover design by 4-9-0 design.
Print Management by Adare Carwin
Printed in Great Britain by J.H. Haynes & Co., Sparkford

Contents

vi *Contents*

Dedication

To the memory of our parents
Thomas and Janette E. Goligher
Dr. Leslie A. and Nora A. Hughes
who faithfully passed on the
'pattern of sound words' they had learned;
who modelled the 'faith and love that are in
Christ Jesus;' and who encouraged us to
'guard the gospel' (2 Tim. 1:13–14).

Introduction

What do you do when sales are down and your product doesn't appear to have the appeal it once had? In the world of business, you may want to re-brand and repackage the product. You may even want to change some of the ingredients and have a re-launch proclaiming that this is a brand new chocolate bar or an 'updated' version of the software.

Apparently this holds true in the world of religion. So when the intellectual climate of the day was denying the supernatural and questioning the origin of the species and rethinking the issues of morality some good evangelical people decided it was time to re-shape the Christian product (the message). They decided that the idea of a God who is holy and who hates sin just didn't play too well in the market of ideas, so they chose to jettison it. They contrived to put together a message that modified sin, reduced God to being 'simply a God of love' and the cross to being a 'demonstration to us of how much God loves us.' So no more original sin, embarrassing wrath, or innocent substitute dying in the place of sinners; it was the 1860s and Liberal theology was born.

As a teenager I was fishing around in a bookstall in The Barrows, Glasgow's famous market, when I discovered a book proclaiming a New Theology. I was fourteen and it cost me 1/6d: I know that because I wrote in it at the time what a waste of money it had been! It recommended dropping such themes as wrath and focusing on the love of God. The main object of horror apparently was the doctrine of the atonement. The idea that sin should be punished in the person of an innocent substitute, our Saviour (the historic Christian position we call penal substitution) was first parodied and then rejected. 'This view of the atonement is unethical, and, in my judgement and that of many others, has wrought a good deal of mischief in the past and bewilderment in the present.'[1] The book was published in 1907 and Modernist theology was on the way in.

Later I was being interviewed by the ministerial recognition committee of a mainstream denomination. I had been required to submit a statement of faith and the college principal had found one particular statement rather amusing. He mocked my commitment to penal substitution and accused me of being an eighteen-year-old dinosaur. Liberal theology was still alive in the 1960s.

What goes around comes around. So in 2003 another book hits the shelves. Its title gave the sense that this was to be new ground-breaking stuff: *The Lost Message of Jesus*.[2] But as I read it I had déjà vu! Here was the same tired old same old. Its importance lies only in that it is an expression of a change that is taking place within the evangelical stream of Christianity. There are people who still claim the title evangelical who are questioning the nature of God. For some it is whether God is in fact 'Almighty.' Others wonder whether he does in fact 'know' the future in any meaningful sense and certainly deny that he controls it. Still others reject the belief that God is Holy and want to reduce his whole being to simply 'love.'

The Bible's teaching on the atonement is also up for grabs. Did Jesus die to pay the penalty for my sins? No, say a number of Christian leaders. They parody this view by portraying the idea of an innocent Son being punished by his Father as a form of child abuse. And still others are rejecting the idea that justification is something that belongs to the beginning of the Christian life. Instead of justification (a right standing with God) being by 'faith alone in Christ alone' it now looks (according to some of the writers of the new perspectives on Paul) as if we are to be justified in the future by works. But does any of this stand up to serious biblical analysis? I believe not.

I have intentionally begun the story of redemption with Jesus himself, with his self-conscious awareness of being God's eternal Son and the Scripture-announced Messiah. In John 17, he gives us an insight into the nature of God as being sovereign (he plans history in detail); holy and righteous (over against the 'world' and 'the evil one') and loving in devising a great plan to redeem his people through the work on earth that Jesus would carry through to the finish. He gives us an insight into his own mind and heart as he talks boldly of the life and love he shared with the Father from all eternity, of his voluntary willingness to undertake to become the world's Redeemer, and of his long-term goal to save and secure the people the Father had given him out of the world. John 17 acts as a curtain raiser to the unfolding drama of redemption which, with its central act the events of Jesus' earthly life, is being played out on the stage of human history and moving towards its final act: Jesus' second coming and the bringing of everything together in him.

Act 1 Scene 1

The message Jesus never lost

Imagine you went to the theatre to see a new play, one you had never seen before. You arrive late, can't find a programme, and sit down somewhere in the middle of Act 4. And you're lost. You can't make sense of who the characters are, what they are doing, how they relate to each other, what they are talking about or what has happened already.

Sometimes we can approach the work of God in the same way. We start from where we are now, and try to make sense of what is going on. And we can make a poor job of it. But we don't need to do that. In the Bible, we have access to the very first scene in the drama – not Genesis, but before time even began. In John 17 we have the very first scene in the very first act of the drama of the redemption – God's plans before the beginning of the world to save humanity from the consequences of its sin.

In verse 5, Jesus refers to a period 'before the world began' or literally before the world existed. Again in verse 24 he refers back to a time 'before the creation of the world.' Here is the Lord Jesus Christ, taking us up to the

throne room of heaven, back to a time before there was
time or space or matter. Here we have a curtain drawn
back so we can hear God's plans. John's message, from
the very beginning of his gospel, was that there was
Someone before creation who was responsible for
everything that is. Of course other religions believe in
one God who is the maker of everything, so what is so
revolutionary about the Christian message? It is that
before there was anything other than God, there was a
relationship.

The relationship that has always existed

The first characters on the stage of our drama are caught
up in the first relationship, which existed before there
was time and space. In John 17 we are eavesdropping on
a prayer that Jesus' disciples were intended to hear and
we were intended to read, which reveals this
relationship. That's why Jesus spoke publicly and loudly
so that they could record what he said. In this prayer, as
John Calvin puts it, 'We see the soul of Jesus'; we see
what his relationship was with the Father. We discover a
relationship in this prayer which we instantly know we
do not have. Jesus' prayer reveals a love relationship at
the heart of the cosmos.

Why is this so important for us? This window into the
heart of God is very significant for our understanding of
who God is. There is only one God but his is not a *simple*
oneness. He is certainly not without emotion, and he has
always had an object to love. It is important for our
understanding of ourselves. Why do we as humans crave
for deep and meaningful relationships? It reflects the fact
that we have been made by a God who enjoys a perfect
relationship in himself, a God who enjoys great love and

wants to share that relationship with us. This is important for the Christian witness to the world. People around us struggle with broken relationships, and the Christian gospel, especially the message of the cross, is all about right relationships.

John's gospel suggests to us that one of the deepest burdens on our Lord's heart during his last hours with his disciples was to help them understand that God's being as Trinity is the heart of what makes the gospel both possible and actual, and that it is knowing him as such that forms the very lifeblood of the life of faith.

The Lord your God is One

Talking about the Trinity is to dive into the deep waters of Christian thought. We may at first think it is way over our heads and therefore not something we need to trouble ourselves about. Yet if we think like that, we will miss something. The Bible is absolutely consistent in declaring that there is only one God. Jews still say the words of the Shema from the Old Testament, 'Hear O Israel, the Lord your God is One' when they gather for synagogue worship.

There is only one God but, because he is God, we should not be surprised to discover that this oneness is a complex oneness. The apostle John captures this in the opening words of his gospel. There he speaks of one God; 'the Word was with God and the Word was God.' The language he uses points to the Word being divine. Yet he does not equate him with the Father. They stand in the closest relation, but they are not identical. Any reading of the rest of John's gospel will show how carefully he balanced the relationship between Father and Son. And the rest of New Testament writers do the same. It's all nuanced so that there is a distinction between the Father and the Son on the one hand, and yet the Father and the Son share an equality that is unique and eternal. We often assume that the oneness of God is a simple oneness. The New Testament leads us to believe in one God, but that is a complex unity, a complex oneness.

You can see this mysterious oneness of God wherever you look in the Bible, even in Genesis 1. There God created the heavens and the earth. A few verses later, the Spirit of God is hovering over the face of the waters. Then we find him speaking to himself as over and over again it says 'and God said'. It is therefore no surprise to discover a mere hint at a complexity within his nature when, at the pinnacle of his creation, he says 'Let us make man in our image, in our likeness' (Gen. 1:26). And the creation of man captures this same complexity: 'so God created man (singular) in his own image, in the image of God (singular) he created him; male and female he created them' (Gen. 1:27).

In John 1:1, this relationship of God is opened up more fully. There are echoes of Genesis: 'In the beginning was the Word . . . and the Word was God'. Then verse 14 says 'the Word became flesh'; he became a human being. And the link between verse 1 and verse 14 is very important. The 'was' of verse 1 contrasts with the 'became' of verse 14. The Word *was* God, the Word *became* flesh. The Word never *became* God, he always was God, but the Word became flesh. There was no beginning to him as God; there was a beginning to him in his humanity.

Later in John, Jesus hints again at his pre-existence. When the Jewish leaders challenge him: 'You are not yet fifty years old, and you have seen Abraham!' Jesus replies that he has seen Abraham, because 'before Abraham was born, I am!' (Jn. 8:57–58). He uses language that presses home the open-endedness of his existence and the words

'I am' relate him in the closest possible way to the God of Israel. When God revealed his name to Moses, he said 'I am who I am . . . "Say this to the people of Israel, 'I am has sent me to you.'"' Jesus self-consciously takes the name of God, and over and over again in John's Gospel he says 'I am': 'before Abraham was, I am'; 'I am the light of the world'; 'I am the good shepherd'; 'I am the resurrection.' No wonder he was so regularly accused of – and finally condemned for – blasphemy.

Throughout John's Gospel there are repeated sayings that emphasise Jesus' self-awareness. 'No one has ascended into heaven except he who descended from heaven, the Son of Man.' 'Then what if you were to see the Son of Man ascending to where he was before?'(Jn. 3:13; 6:62). These refer to the ascension, which was not to be a new experience for Jesus but a return to what he had been familiar with before.

Abba Father

Four times in this prayer in John 17, Jesus addresses God as 'Father'(Jn. 17:1; 5; 21; 24). The Aramaic word means 'daddy' or 'dear father.' There is no precedent for it being used to address God for the simple reason that it would have seemed overfamiliar to use the language of a tiny child or a mature adult to their beloved father. But Jesus uses it all the time, except for his cry of dereliction on the cross. The language is all familiarity and intimacy. Throughout John's Gospel, we find Jesus delighting in this description of himself as the Son, and in talking to God as his Father. And John sees the whole purpose of his book as proclaiming Jesus' sonship: 'These are written so that you may believe that Jesus is the Christ, the Son of God'(Jn. 20:31). To be God's Son is to share God's nature and to be one with him: 'I and the Father are one.'

This Son is unique because he is eternal and uncreated. He is Son by nature while human beings become children of God only by adoption. In fact, it is only as we believe in the Son that we are given the right 'to become children of God' (Jn. 1:12). This Son exercises divine powers and prerogatives. He claims to be equal with God: that to see him is to see the Father; that we are to believe in him as we are to believe in God; and that he and the Father are one. It is no surprise, then, that after the resurrection Thomas responds to the risen Christ with the words, 'My Lord and my God' (Jn. 20:28). Augustine wrote: 'I can see the depths of God, but I cannot see the bottom.'

The love of Father and Son

Chapter 17 is all about the love that exists between the Father and the Son, and the Son to the Father. In verse 24 for example he says, 'You loved me before the creation of the world.' At the very end of the chapter he prays that his people would be with them in glory and that they might experience the love that they have always had for each other. One of the amazing things we discover about John 17 is that it is not an exclusive or selfish love; it is a giving love. Here is the unique Christian understanding of God, that his love has always been other-oriented. Through his plurality-in-unity, he has always been able to express his love within his own being. We find it hard to get our minds around that but it is tremendously reassuring to know that God, who enjoys perfect love within himself, wants to share that with the creatures he has made.

Self-giving is the opposite of our kind of love. Very often we draw out of others what we need but this love gives and gives again. So we discover Jesus' people drawn into this love. Verse 23 says 'You sent me, and have loved them even as you have loved me.' Verse 26; '... that the love you have for me may be in them and I myself may be in them.' The passion that develops in this chapter is almost like two concentric circles, moving in opposite directions. First of all the Father loves believers and the believers love the Son. And the Son loves the Father. Then the Father loves the Son and the Son loves the believers and the believers love the Son in response. Love is built into the fabric of the chapter. This love is ours through our connection with his well-loved Son. And believers throughout history have delighted in such love. John Calvin goes into raptures in describing the generous mercy by which God acts in Christ to deal with our sin so that 'there might be no obstruction to his love.'[3]

It has been suggested that 'God is love' is the complete truth about God, but that is not so, as far as the Bible is concerned. In this chapter I want you to notice how the Son describes the Father. He is not only Dear Father. Twice in this chapter he acknowledges that the Father is both holy and righteous. Look at verse 11: even to the Lord Jesus, he is the Holy Father. Verse 25, he is the 'Righteous father'. We are all unholy and unrighteous by the Bible's definition. And there is judgement in this chapter amongst all the expressions of love. There is one individual described as the son of destruction, Judas Iscariot. And there is hostility to God, there is the hostility of the world that hates God and his word and is under his judgement. This Father that Jesus refers to is the Holy and Righteous One whom we have offended.

This connects up with the unfolding revelation of God in all the Bible. God made the world then judged it by the Flood; he called Abraham and made him a great nation, then disciplined that nation through conquest, captivity and exile; he sent his Son into the world to save the world and he will one day send that same Son to be its Judge. So

God's love is not the complete truth about God as far as the Bible is concerned but it is the complete truth about God as far as the Christian is concerned. The world remains in hostility to God and liable to his judgement. On the other hand, Jesus prays for those God has given him and asks that they might be kept by the power of God from the evil one and one day see his glory. Sin has led to brokenness, alienation and the death of love. Through Christ, there is the prospect of a restored and deepening friendship with God and confidence in his presence.

The plan that has always existed

So what are the main characters in our drama discussing, in this first scene of the first act?

They're talking about something which has been planned in detail before the foundation of the world. We rarely hear people talk about the plan of redemption. In fact some would have us think that God was working today without any kind of script at all, that God was simply a reacting figure somewhere in the universe; guessing what we are going to do next but not really knowing and then responding as best he can, trying to retrieve something good from the failures and messes that we make (This view is called Open Theism.)

That isn't the picture that we have here. God is not the God of Open Theism. He is a God who has a plan, and God the Father is the Author of this plan. This is crucial to grasp today. Throughout Scripture, redemption comes from God's love. God chose Israel because he loved her, not because of her intrinsic worth. The salvation spoken of in the New Testament is the Father's idea. The Christian gospel doesn't start with Jesus; it starts with

God the Father. The giving of the Son is the proof that 'God so loved the world' (Jn. 3:16). And the giving of people to the Son is evidence that the Father loves them as he loves his Son (Jn. 17:23). As Jesus talks to his Father, he is talking about the work that the Father gave him to do (v4).

The New Testament doesn't go into great detail about how this works. It is clear that each member of the Trinity is equal in being and power, yet there is an order. The Bible's order is Father, Son and Holy Spirit. And whenever the New Testament is talking about our salvation, it invariably describes it as the gift of God, entirely of God from beginning to end. Right from the beginning, we are being led to see that there is nothing humanity can do: it is utterly helpless to save or help itself. The gospel is more than simply a proposal God has outlined; the gospel plan is put in place before there were any people to save. Right from the beginning of the drama there was a plan – salvation wasn't brought in as an emergency measure following the fall. From the beginning it is the good news of what God has purposed to do for his people. It begins with God alone in glory and it ends with us seeing and sharing the glory of God.

The *purpose* of redemption was the salvation of a people out of the world. The 'world' is not a nice place in John's gospel or anywhere else in the New Testament. It is the place where people are in revolt against God, hostile to God and to God's people. It organises itself without reference to God. It lies in the power of the evil one and the people in it are going to perish because they are 'condemned already' (Jn. 3:16–21). That God should love the world is almost incredible to those who begin to see it as God sees it. The need of the world is to be made right with this Righteous Father, to be reconciled to him. It needs to receive eternal life, since the lives of its people are forfeit because of their rebellion. Out of the world God has chosen a people 'those you have given him,' the people 'you gave me out of the world' (Jn. 17:2; 6; 9) and we know that this is an international company made up of people from every age, race and language.

The *mediator* **of redemption** is Jesus himself. Look at what Jesus has said in verse 2: God has 'granted him authority over all people'. A mediator is someone who stands between two parties, able to touch both sides in an argument, standing in the gap between the offenders and offended. The word isn't used here in John 17 but it's used everywhere else and this is the role that Jesus has been given: God granted him authority over all people. Jesus is made the head and the Redeemer of his people.

The *focus* **of redemption** is the cross. In fact, the New Testament typically defines love by reference to the cross. That is the crisis that provokes this prayer in the first place. Like any human being facing execution, Jesus' mind is concentrated on what lies ahead and he wants to talk to his Father about it. But what amazes us is to learn that this was a subject they had planned and discussed before the world was made. In fact there was a carefully planned timetable of events. In verse 1 he says, 'Father, the hour has come' (ESV). We know from John's gospel that this 'hour' was on Jesus' mind from the beginning of his public ministry. Right at the beginning of his ministry, in Cana of Galilee, Jesus' mother Mary asked him to act when the wine ran out at a wedding. Maybe she wanted him to show himself as the Messiah she knew him to be. Instead, he reminds her that their relationship is different now that he has begun his public ministry. As the Son of Man, his task was to bring the realities of heaven into people's lives. So he tells her, 'My hour is not yet come' (Jn. 2:4 ESV).

Five times in John's Gospel he says 'My hour (or my time) has not yet come' (Jn. 2:4; 7:6, 8, 30; 8:20 ESV). But as the cross comes into view, in John 12:23, he says 'The hour has come for the Son of Man to be glorified.' And he then goes straight on to talk of 'a grain of wheat' which falls to the ground and dies, before it can bear 'much fruit.' He will not be diverted from 'this hour' in spite of his 'soul' being 'troubled' (Jn.12:27 ESV). As they gather in the upper room, we are told 'Jesus knew that his hour had come to depart out of the world to the Father' (Jn.13:1 ESV). Is God taken by surprise? Does this sound like a God who acts without a script, as Open Theism would teach us? Doesn't it sound as if the whole of history and the work of Christ have been scripted, down to the minutest detail of timing? In fact, Peter on the Day of Pentecost is able to declare that Jesus was 'delivered up according to the definite plan and foreknowledge of God'(Acts 2:23 ESV).

The whole ministry of Jesus moves up to this point. He sees the cross as his reason for coming into the world in the first place. As he speaks to his Father, it is the cross that is uppermost in his mind. He reflects on the plan of redemption, and the outcome of this cross-work in the rescue of many people. So committed is he to the task that he is able to speak as if he has already been there and finished the job. 'I glorified you on earth, accomplishing the work that you gave me to do' (Jn.17:4).

The *way* of redemption is to 'know you, the only true God, and Jesus Christ, whom you have sent' (Jn.17:3). There is no hint of that doctrine of universalism that teaches there are many ways to God. There is no embarrassment in Jesus' voice as he unashamedly declares the uniqueness of the way he offers to men. He has already made this point to his disciples in John 14:6, 'I am the way, and the truth, and the life. No one comes to the Father except through me' (ESV).

This plan is sometimes called the eternal covenant. In Ephesians 3:11 the Apostle Paul talks about God's 'eternal purpose that he has realised in Christ Jesus our Lord' (ESV). Here the Greek word translated 'purpose' can also mean 'plan' or 'resolve.' God has one overarching purpose or plan. It is eternal. He has always had a plan. And the person and work of Christ are central to God's eternal plan because it says that God realised, 'accomplished' or 'effected' it, literally, 'in the Christ, Jesus our Lord.'[4] Christ is God's Alpha and Omega, the beginning, centre and the goal of his eternal purpose. His intention is to 'unite all things in him, things in heaven and things on earth' (Eph. 1:10).

Is it possible for us as Christians ever to talk too much about the cross? To suggest this demonstrates a complete misunderstanding of the whole movement of God's purposes in history and the great mission of Jesus' own life, *as he himself saw it*! Those who have argued that the cross should not be as central as it has been to our preaching have not understood that the gospels are all preliminary to the cross. The cross is the action; everything else is leading up to the action of the cross. We preach Christ crucified. What was in Jesus' mind here in this prayer? It is the cross. That is what Jesus is thinking about when he says in verse 4: 'I have glorified you on earth, by completing the work that you gave me to do.' The word he uses there, he will use once more, when he's on the cross and cries in a loud voice 'Finished!' That's why he had come into the world.

The goal that always existed

'Glorify your Son, that your Son may glorify you.' The Westminster Catechism asked the question 'What is the chief end of man?' and the answer was, 'The chief end of man is to glorify God and enjoy him forever.' The goal of redemption is to bring us to the place where *we* want what Jesus *wants* here: the glory of God. The essence of sin is that we will not glorify God. Every Christian will either have a God-centred or a man-centred theology. The Christian who gives the Bible its due will learn that, just as the chief end of man is to glorify God and to enjoy him forever, so also *the chief end of God* is to glorify *himself* and to enjoy *himself* forever. He will learn from Scripture that God loves himself with a holy love and with all his heart, soul, mind, and strength, and that he himself is the centre of his affections, and that the impulse that drives him and the thing he pursues in everything he does is his own glory![5]

So before we think about the benefits of salvation to us, we need to say that first of all it was God's intention to glorify himself in the salvation of his people. We are creatures, he is the Creator. We are contingent beings, dependent on other things; God is not contingent on anything. He is the highest good in the universe. This is Jesus' clear agenda as he comes to his Father and faces the cross: 'Father the time has come. Glorify your son, that your son may glorify you.' Jesus never lost his message: he knew what it was right to the very end, and he saw himself and his work at the heart of the plan. The same emphasis is taken up by the Apostle Paul in Ephesians 1, where he speaks of the 'purpose of his will,' which is being worked out in time 'to the praise of his glorious grace' and (twice) 'to the praise of his glory' (Eph. 1:6, 12, 14 ESV).

What do we mean by the glory of God? It would be true to say that the world does not understand the idea of glory. I think of the cynicism expressed by Bertrand Russell before his death, when he said:

No dungeon was ever constructed so dark and narrow as that in which the shadow physics of our time imprisons us, for every prisoner has believed that outside his walls a free world existed; but now the prison has become the whole universe. *There is darkness without, and when I die there will be darkness within. There is no splendour, no vastness anywhere, only triviality* for a moment and then nothing.[6]

But here something contradicts all that. Before the universe there was *a vastness* – God himself. And there was the *splendour* we call the 'glory' of God. Jesus refers to 'the glory I had with you before the world existed' (Jn. 17.5 ESV). He yearns to go home to his Father. Before there was space and time there was the vastness and splendour of God himself. And there is the opposite of triviality. There is *weight*. Glory is something that has weight. It is 'heavy' – there is nothing light or lightweight about God or about his salvation. But it is also splendid, full of brightness and beauty.

What about those who appear to have lost confidence in the gospel today? They jettison the uncomfortable parts of Jesus' teaching to make it more acceptable to the masses. The motivation is to keep Christianity from declining and dying by absorbing as much of the world's agenda as we can, by making us as much like the world as we can, but still calling ourselves Christian. All of us want to be popular with our neighbours and colleagues but we find it hard to sit down and talk about things such as sin, judgement and hell. I have no doubt about the compassionate motive of many such folk and their desire to reach our generation for Christ. But they give away too much and end up sacrificing the gospel of God on the altar of expediency.

The great goal that lies behind the universe of space and time is the display of the splendour and worth of

God, the display of his glory. The final proof of our salvation is that we will want God to be glorified. This is Jesus' priority here. Before he goes to the cross, before he prays for our salvation and preservation (which he does later) he prays that God will be glorified.

This chapter begins and ends with the glory of God. From one point of view, it points us back to a time when God enjoyed his glory himself. Father and Son delighted in each other. But at the end of this chapter we have this startling revelation that Jesus intends that his people should *see and share* his glory. That is God's great goal. And, if we may dare make such a statement, God reckons that everything in between – everything in human experience and history – 'all these present sufferings' are 'not worth comparing with the glory that is going to be revealed in us.' With this inspiration, for the joy set before him, Jesus endured the cross, despising the shame.

Act 1 Scene 2

East of Eden

The first scene of the first act of the drama of redemption has been played. Plans have been made to redeem people and bring them to glory. But we don't know why people are going to need that salvation provision so desperately. To discover that, we need to come out of the theatre and look around us.

There is something wrong with humanity. Our newspapers are filled with stories of fraudulent practices in business, of celebrities' serial marriages, brutal rapes, whole populations descending into violence and looting as soon as the restraints of law and order are withdrawn. We see the problem with humanity at work in our own families sometimes, as we rub each other up the wrong way.

So why is there something wrong with humanity? Scene 2 of our drama takes place in a Garden and provides the answer, and the script is from Genesis 3, which takes us to the very beginning of the human story and what God is doing in the world. Genesis 3 is Holy Scripture and authentic history. That is the way that the

New Testament views it, and as Christians we are bound by the New Testament to view it as Christ and the apostles viewed it. Genesis gives us many answers to what is revealed elsewhere in the Bible. And Old Testament scholar, Derek Kidner, says

> Genesis, in fact, is in various ways almost nearer to the New Testament than the Old, and some of its topics are barely heard again till their implications can fully emerge in the gospel. The institution of marriage, the Fall of man, the jealousy of Cain, the judgement of the Flood, the imputed righteousness of the believer, the rival sons of promise and of the flesh, the profanity of Esau, the pilgrim status of God's people, are all predominantly New Testament themes.[7]

Everything in the Garden is rosy

As the curtain goes up on Scene 2, a gasp runs round the audience. Never have they seen such a superb, beautiful scene. This is total, overwhelming perfection. The Bible begins by describing a universe that is created by God, and it is perfect in every detail.

There are three ways of looking at the universe that we live in. Some see the universe as *open* – open to all kind of supernatural involvement; an open universe where spirits control everything and we are at the mercy of their whims. They are unpredictable and you cannot foretell what they are going to do, so science is impossible in an open universe.

In reaction, the scientists posit a *closed* universe. Everything can be explained by cause and effect at a purely material level. Science is possible: God is excluded. Reading Richard Dawkins or Stephen

Hawking will show the religious fervour with which this view of a closed universe is held. The Bible, however, teaches a *controlled* universe. Don Carson defines it thus

> A controlled universe reflected in the Bible has God as both its Creator and its sustainer/ruler. He creates in an ordered way; he sustains and rules it in an ordered way so that science is possible. But he is not bound by what he has created, so he is at perfect liberty to do things another way, with the result that miracles are possible.[8]

Genesis teaches us that we live in a controlled universe, and everything about God's creation is good. The whole created process in chapter 1 is aimed at the foreseen good. Light is proclaimed to be good. So are the lands and the sea, the fruitfulness of the earth, the great heavenly bodies: and the whole process is crowned by the making of human beings, male and female. God says humanity is very good. The Genesis account begins with perfect people in a perfect environment.

And it wasn't just the environment and the people who were perfect – so was the place and the purpose. Genesis was written by Moses, and first read by Israelites just after they had been taken out of Egypt, wandering round in the desert for forty years, never reaching the Promised Land. They are in the wilderness of Sinai, and it is barren, rugged, like a lunar landscape. Nothing is growing and it lacks almost every kind of life, with few plants. But as they read the Genesis account, they see that originally the world was a paradise. A river runs through this paradise, which is full of precious metals; there is gold everywhere, and as the children of Israel read this, they are thinking – 'Here we are, in a barren desert, with no running water, no resources. This is where Adam and his sin has landed us.'

Created for his glory

Why did God make people in the first place? For the making of everything was not to be an end in itself. Everything that is made derives its meaning and existence from the God who made it. God speaks in Isaiah of those 'whom I created for my glory, whom I formed and made' (Is. 43:7). Here are perfect people in a perfect environment with a perfect purpose: to glorify God in their work, in their relationships and in their play. In John 17, the Lord Jesus is preoccupied in his prayer with the glory of God: 'Father, the time has come. Glorify your Son, that your Son may glorify you.' That was Jesus' passion. Jesus wants the splendour of God to be seen, the value of God to be appreciated and the name of God to be known. God makes people and the world so that he might be glorified. As the Westminster Catechism says 'The chief end of man is to glorify God and enjoy him forever.'

But how do we glorify God? We glorify God by obeying him perfectly. In John 17, Jesus says, 'I have brought you glory on earth by completing the work you gave me to do.' Jesus glorified God by doing the work God gave him to do. Will man do the same?

Man on trial

Man is put in the garden and given a work by God, to have dominion over everything, to name the animals and to enjoy a relationship with God. There is only one 'but': God says, 'You are free to eat from any tree in the garden; but you must not eat from the tree of the knowledge of good and evil, for when you eat of it you will surely die' (Gen. 2:16, 17).

God puts two trees in the garden in the midst of all the others. Life was at the centre of this Garden. There is a 'tree of life' and by eating of it, humans could live forever. The other tree, the tree of the knowledge of good and evil, is a test: the only test in the entire universe for Adam and Eve. They are on probation in the garden. The test is not given to trip them up but to give them the opportunity to choose God's way freely. It is a very real test and the mention of these trees brings home the tragedy of what is to come.

This arrangement is often called the covenant of works or the covenant of life. The word isn't used here, though it is called a covenant in Hosea 6:7: 'Like Adam, they have broken the covenant – they were unfaithful to me there.' A covenant is an arrangement between a superior and a minor power and all the ingredients are here. The two *parties* in this agreement are God and man. There is a *promise* of eternal life or death; there are *benefits* – Adam and Eve have been given everything in the universe to use and they can eat of any tree in the garden. But there is one *condition*. Of all the trees of the garden, there is one they cannot eat from. And finally, there is a *curse*: if they do eat from the forbidden tree, then the curse of death will come into play – death for disobedience.

Adam and Eve sign up for this special relationship, this covenant, with all its terms and conditions. Here are two creatures with absolute freedom of choice given the simplest choice in the most favourable of surroundings, and at this stage there is not one cloud in the sky, not one skeleton in the closet, nothing to obscure the simplicity of the choice.

Why are they given this test? People can tell you that they love you and will do anything for you. The real test of whether they love you is when there is a challenge to that love. Do you see the issue? Will free creatures, who have everything they could possibly want, love God freely if they are given an alternative?

There's a snake in the garden

Then a new figure slithers onto the stage – the serpent. If this was a pantomime, the audience would be hissing. But it is far too serious for that. The serpent is a literal creature, under the rule of the devil, and he is going to attack humanity. But his attack on humanity is an attack on his real enemy – God.

The first thing the serpent does is to distort God's word. He asks 'Did God really say?' or as the ESV puts it, 'Did God actually say "You shall not eat of any tree in the garden?"' God didn't actually say that, and Eve recognises that that's not what God said, and so she corrects him. She says to the serpent, 'We may eat of the fruit of the trees in the garden, but God said "You shall not eat of the fruit of the tree that's in the midst of the garden."' Firstly, she's minimising God's kindness, as if being able to eat from every tree but one was some kind of denial on God's part. Then she adds to God's word, 'neither shall you touch it, lest you die.' God never said that, but now she's thinking of God as being particularly strict. We often exaggerate the hardness of God's commands.

The serpent is subtle, and he's put Eve in the place of authority. She's now an expert on religious matters, jumping in to correct him. But she has also had her attention drawn to God's prohibition, and realises, perhaps for the very first time, that she is restricted by another. That's why she adds the word 'neither shall you touch it.' She is now open to the thought that God may be restricting her too severely.

The devil or the serpent can now build on her distortion. 'You will not surely die,' he says. What he's implying is 'God is being selfish, threatening your potential. God knows that if you eat of that tree you will be equal with him. Your eyes will be open, you will acquire the knowledge of good and evil, you will become like God.' He is flatly denying the idea that God would ever judge sin with death. It's interesting that it is the doctrine of judgement that is the very first to be denied. It frequently still is.

So what happens? Eve disobeys, defying God's word. She saw 'that the fruit of the tree was good for food and pleasing to the eye . . . she took some and ate it.' She ate what she was told not to eat. It was the action that was a sign and seal of the change that has taken place in Eve's heart. With that act things go downhill at breakneck speed: 'she also gave some to her husband, who was with her, and he ate' (3:6a). Eve may well have been deceived but Adam sinned with his eyes wide open and instantly both became covenant breakers.

What actually happens in this scene, in the Fall? Our first parents allow Satan to challenge God's word and remain silent in the face of his lie that they 'will not surely die.' They show a willingness to reject God's authority over them. They allow Satan to reduce God's word to a mere hypothesis at best, and a lie at worst. They choose human autonomy over God's authority. You see the Fall *is* a big deal. It matters. The New Testament says this: 'Sin came into the world through one man, and death spread to all men because all sinned.' We have lived with the effects ever since.

Paradise Lost

What are the implications of this sin for Adam and Eve? Hiding behind a fig leaf isn't just a bit of fun: it is a real attempt to relieve their shame and rid themselves of the guilt they now feel. Anyone who has ever felt ashamed will recognise the symptoms. It is shame that drives them to flee when God comes looking for them. And when God does come, he says to Adam, 'Who told you that you were naked?' Adam and Eve are now sinners, and one sin leads to another. They won't take the blame, they blame one another, then they blame the devil, and finally they imply that it is God's fault for getting them into this mess. And humans have been blaming God for their problems ever since.

Adam and Eve face a breakdown in their relationship with each other, and a bigger breakdown in their relationship with God. God sentences them to death and throws them out of the Garden, which (the chapter goes on to tell us) is forever closed by a flaming sword, the symbol of God's justice, and policed by the cherubim, the guardians of God's holiness.

Is that the end of the fallout? No: the environment is also cursed. 'Cursed is the ground because of you,' says God to the man. Everything is cursed because of man's disobedience: animals and nature are caught up into the mess of our parents' disobedience. Back then, right down the whole length of Africa was thick forest. Right across what is now the Middle East, down the Saudi Peninsula, right over to India was a thick forest and fertile land, all to be denuded by men, bringing about ecological breakdown. We see the same thing happening now in South America. Humans have caused untold ecological damage and it all stems from this one event: man's sin in the Garden and man's sin ever since.

The fallout goes into the animal kingdom as well. Sharks attack seals and whales attack sea lions, and cats attack birds. All of nature is out of joint. Paul says in Romans 8 that all of creation had been subjected to futility. Then there are the volcanoes, earthquakes, tornadoes and the fires that appear to rage out of control. Finally, we see the fallout in humanity itself. All of those global disasters stem from this one event.

Eve will suffer pain in childbirth and have this driving desire to try and master her husband. Where there was once harmony amongst the sexes, now there is competition. Adam is sentenced to painful toil, struggling for existence. Both are destined to die. Death is an alien intruder into God's good world. 'Dust you are, and to dust you will return.' This is the penal aspect to the fallout. Adam and Eve and their posterity are sentenced to death. The New Testament says that 'the wages of sin is death' (Rom. 6:23). In order to bring home this judicial curse, both are banished from the Garden of Eden, to work the ground. Even in chapter 4:14, Cain their son is aware of this judicial sentence after he murders his brother and he says, 'I am hidden from your presence.' To sin is both to die and to be banished from the presence of God.

Death becomes the common denominator of all of Adam's descendants. One after another, following the first fratricide, Genesis recounts 'and he died . . . and he died . . . and he died'. Sin is radical in its effects, and within a few generations it has spread throughout the body of humanity. Genesis 6:5 says 'The LORD saw how great man's wickedness on the earth had become, and that every inclination of the thoughts of his heart was only evil all the time.' So whatever recovery operation God has to put in place, it has to deal with death, the penalty that hangs over humanity. It has to deal with the sin problem within us and it has to resolve the problem of the estrangement of humanity from its Maker. It has to bring people back to God. It has to open a way to Paradise.

How does this fit into God's plan? Did this turn of events take God by surprise? The Bible forbids us to think that God is the first cause of evil. Yet he did make human beings with freedom to choose. And freedom of choice, to be real, must include a choice away from God as well as a choice for him.

If we are going to be strictly biblical, there are two things that we have to affirm here. Firstly, God does ordain whatever comes to pass. In other words, God is the sole cause of everything. The Bible doesn't hide from that reality. Secondly, the Bible says God cannot be charged with causing sin. It insists that God is light and in him there is no darkness at all, and that he tempts no-one to sin.

God is the author of everything but he is not the author of sin. So how does this work? In the Westminster Confession of Faith it uses this expression: that God 'works his will in accordance with the nature of second causes.' So God works his will out in our planet, within the system of the orbit of the earth round the sun and the movements of the galaxies. He doesn't interfere with them; he operates within that context. Similarly he made human beings, and he works on the basis of making free human beings, with free will, to choose good or bad. He never tampers with that free will. He allows us our free, totally spontaneous ability to make decisions, and he works with that ability.

He also works in a way so that there are contingencies. For example, sometimes he warns people 'If you do this, this will happen; if you do that, that will happen.' God warned the people of Nineveh in the book of Jonah and said 'If you repent, God will forgive you. If you don't, judgement will come.'

Adam and Eve were aware of God's prohibition over eating the fruit. They had the power to do God's will but they made their own choice. God didn't interfere with their decision. They sinned willingly, spontaneously, without pressure exerted on them by God, and yet in spite of that, everything they did was comprehended by the will and the purpose of God. After his brothers hated and sold him, Joseph said, 'You meant evil against me, but God meant it for good.' Stephen said something similar when he spoke to the people of Jerusalem and said, 'This Jesus who was delivered up by the determined plan and foreknowledge of God, you crucified and killed.' You did it but it came within God's plan and purpose. God works out his plan according to the nature of second causes. He lets us do our thing but all the time he is overruling our decisions, even working through our bad decisions to achieve his purpose. His will is done most surely. God is the author of all things, either by his positive ordering or by his active concurrence. Everything that happens serves his purpose and his plan.

Man is facing a test of love and he fails the test. He is out of the garden. But this scene doesn't finish with condemnation – instead it contains the first hint in Genesis of the gospel. What is humanity's great need at this point? It is grace. To be shown it is the most surprising part of the story, yet we find grace proclaimed here. Grace has to do with the most unlikely response possible. Where there should be wrath, there is love shown.

The first gospel

'I will put enmity between you and the woman, and between your offspring and her offspring; he shall bruise your head, and you shall bruise his heel' (Gen. 3:15). This is what Martin Luther called the *protevangelium* – the first gospel proclamation. This verse is not about why people don't like snakes!

Who is the *seed*, the 'offspring of the woman' or the 'seed of the woman?' This is the beginning of a theme that will develop throughout the Bible. The word seed is singular and implies an individual, rather than a corporate, fulfilment. The idea reappears elsewhere in the Bible; we read about *Abraham's* 'seed;' *David's* 'seed;' the *virgin's* 'seed;' and the *servant's* 'seed'(Gen. 12). Those nearest to the promise understood it as an individual who would help reverse the effects of the Fall. So Adam and Eve named their son Seth, which means 'appointing,' 'God has appointed for me another offspring instead of Abel, for Cain killed him' (4:25), taking up the promise of 3:15. Lamech nourishes the hope of a promised 'seed' in his son Noah. The promised offspring would resolve the problem brought about by sin. God is declaring that he will provide a Redeemer. This appointed one would be mortally wounded but he would finally destroy Satan's kingdom of evil.

Who is the *serpent*, the enemy of God and humanity?

He is not treated as an animal in the story. Snakes were regarded as part of God's good creation. The serpent is not part of that creation, for it is not an animal pure and simple and it is certainly not 'good.' And the serpent is not described as 'it' but as 'he' so that the woman enters into conversation with another person. The serpent is the usurper of the divine right to direct the creation, the corrupter of the word of God, who denies the truth of divine judgment on sin and rebellion, the deceiver of humankind, the author and instigator of a fallen creation – destined, at last, to be crushed.

In the book of Revelation, written by the same John who records the prayer of Jesus, we find a deliberate allusion to this chapter. The serpent is identified: he is none other than Satan (Rev. 12:9). 'That ancient serpent . . . the devil or Satan.' In Revelation, the shoe fits. He is the one who opposes the work of God; a murderer, deciever and liar; committed to destroying reverence for the word of God, removing the fear of sin and overthrowing the integrity of the character of God. All these are the targets in Genesis 3. In 3:13 he is called the deciever, 'the serpent decieved me,' says Eve. And in verses 4–5 he slanders the character of God by suggesting that God has unworthy motives in forbidding them to eat from the tree. The movement of the verse is towards a single combat situation and in the cross, Satan meets his nemesis. The Redeemer is wounded but Satan is crushed.

The clothing of Adam and Eve is not incidental to the story. This is God's remedy for the obstacle in their approach to him. It symbolises God's purpose to restore men to fellowship with him. The shame they felt was a religious problem, how they felt in God's presence. It could only be resolved by God and not by their own efforts. Therefore God takes away their fig leaves and gives them proper clothes. Nor is it coincidence that their first clothes involve the death of an innocent animal. They are under the threat of death, and before they themselves die, another creature dies instead and they are covered with its skin and their religious problem is solved by God.

Who will help us?

Whatever else Genesis 3 teaches, it teaches this: that if humanity's problem with God is ever to be resolved, then something has to be done about the judicial curse under which we now live; the penalty of death which hangs over us. The judgement of God has to be faced and removed. We cannot avoid it. Genesis 3 is a direct challenge to those who deny that there is a penal or judgemental aspect to our human dilemma. In fact, it teaches us that it is this very thing that goes to the heart of our need.

Did Adam understand the promise given to him? It is there in the text. He called his wife Eve, which means 'mother of the living.' After the sentence of death has been given, he calls her *life*. It does sound like Adam understood precisely what God was saying in Genesis 3:15. Derek Kidner says, 'Adam heard the promise of Genesis 3:15 in faith, and so he called his wife Eve.' If lost paradise is ever to be restored, then God must do it.

The lessons of Genesis 3 still stand. If we will do all the will of God, we will be saved. But we neither do, nor will to do, all the will of God. Yet this is what Jesus comes to do. In the first place he comes as a second Adam, the leader of a new race. He starts his public life in a desert, not a garden, being tempted by the devil. But he resists where Adam collapsed. He freely puts himself under the law of God as our representative. He meets every demand of God on our behalf. Not only that, because we have violated God's law we have lost eternal life. We are in the realm of the dying, and we are separated from God and under his curse. But Christ comes to take the curse for us, to take our place and experiences in himself the full force of the wrath aimed at us. So now there is but one way to be right with God, the way of faith in Christ the Redeemer.

Act 1 Scene 3

Wet, wet, wet!

Christians are often accused by others of creating God in their own image. It is said that we feel a need for security, for certainty or for love, and we construct a divine figure that will fill those needs. Yet the irony is that it is often people who wouldn't claim to be Christians who are most prone to make God in their image. They say such things as 'I like to see God as . . .' Or 'The God I believe in wouldn't do this, that or the other thing.' Or 'I like to think that a God of love would never do X, Y or Z.' In the end their God is no more than a magnified version of themselves. Are they right?

Having started the drama in John 17, in Scene 1, it is there we need to return – it is the lens through which we see everything else. Listen to the Lord Jesus at this most intimate point in his life: with death facing him, his mind is totally clear. He has no doubt as to what the issues are: why he is here, where he is going, what his message is and what his work is to do. He not only talks to God as his Father but he defines God in terms of righteousness and holiness. If those two words mean anything, they mean that he is setting God over everything that is unholy and unrighteous. Jesus refuses to pray for the world, which he sees as hostile to him and his people and under the control of the evil one.

The scene in this chapter is set in Genesis 6. But why look in the Old Testament? The reason is that Jesus himself consistently looked to the Old Testament to frame his own view of redemption and his part in it.

Beginning in Genesis 4, there is the development of two distinct lines within the human race. There are those who 'call on the name of the Lord' (Gen. 4:26) and there are those who don't. Augustine described them in these terms: 'There are two cities formed by two loves: the earthly by the love of self, even to the contempt of God; the heavenly by the love of God, even to the contempt of self.'[9]

People at this stage live for incredibly long times, and all of them, without exception, die. And in chapter 6, we have a new character on stage – Noah. Jesus himself refers to the days of Noah and draws a parallel with the days before his second coming and the final judgement. He taught that there was something instructive in the record of those days.

The radical corruption of man

What has been happening in the days of Noah? The population had increased, and corruption increased as well. Verse 5: 'The Lord saw how great man's wickedness on the earth had become and that every inclination of the thoughts of his own heart was only evil all the time.' What is going on in this opening part of the chapter?

There are two things: first there has been a crossing of God-given limits. Verse 2 says 'the sons of God saw that the daughters of men were beautiful, and they married any of them they chose.' There are a number of ideas about what this means. There is Calvin's view, that the sons of God are those who come from the godly line mentioned above, and that the people of God were marrying the people of the world, and the identity of God's people was being lost as a result. The other main view is that the reference to the sons of God here (elsewhere in the Old Testament referring to angels) is speaking about fallen angels. This is part of the devil's strategy to destroy the image of God in humanity by polluting the stream of humanity by these unnatural unions, probably by demon possession.

Either way, Satan's hope is to stop the coming of the Saviour promised in Genesis 3:15. There he is called the crusher, for he will crush Satan's head. Satan doesn't want that to happen and wants to destroy this coming one. God could not be born of a demon-possessed mother. Peter may be referring to this in his letter when he talks about Christ 'put to death in the body but made alive by the Spirit, through whom also he went and preached to the spirits in prison who disobeyed long ago when God waited patiently in the days of Noah while the ark was being built' (1 Pet. 3:18–20). Again 2 Peter 2:4 says, 'For . . . God did not spare angels when they sinned, but sent them to hell, putting them into gloomy dungeons to be held for judgement.'

There were unnatural unions, they transgressed God-given limits and they produced superhuman offspring. They are described as the 'Nephilim' in verse 4: 'The Nephilim were on the earth in those days'. They became 'heroes of old, men of renown.' This may very well be the historical basis for the many mythologies of the world, which have a certain pattern to them – they all have stories about half-human, half-divine figures that have occult powers, whether you look at Roman, Greek or Norse mythology. Homer embellished some of these stories, but they probably reflect a racial memory of these outstanding pre-flood people. God did not preserve the ancient world, but preserved Noah.

Along with the crossing of God-given boundaries is a polluting of the God-given image. When God made man in the beginning, male and female, he created them and he breathed into them his Spirit and he pronounced them as very good. But that was no longer true. Verse 5 says 'Every inclination of the thoughts of his heart was only evil all the time.' This can be called either radical corruption or total depravity, although the latter phrase can be misunderstood. Total doesn't mean that people are as bad as they could be, simply that sin goes all the way through. They are not bad all the time.

In the film *Crash* a racist policeman delights to humiliate a woman of mixed race married to an African-American man. She is justifiably angered and frightened by the incident. She is disgusted with her husband for not taking action. But he has learned over the years not to rock the boat. Later this same woman is trapped in an overturned car which is about to explode and finds herself being rescued, at considerable risk to his own life, by the same policeman. Humanity is capable of the most heroic acts of selfishness and selflessness. Our best is always spoiled by our essentially sinful nature.

Christian agencies have been quietly working in Africa over many, many years trying to establish an economic system for people whereby the short-term needs are met, as well as the long-term concerns. Occasionally problems happen that require governments as well as individuals to take action. And from time to time, corrupt regimes siphon off aid. This is a reality. Nor can we ignore the fact that mixed in with the altruism of the many that push the

relief campaign in the West are those who know that a
little bit of publicity won't hurt their careers. Our best
works are shot through with mixed motives and sometimes we give money not just to alleviate hunger but also
to alleviate our own consciences.

By using the words 'total' or 'radical' we are not saying
that everyone is equally bad: we are admitting that sin
has invaded and affected every part of our humanity. It
reaches to the very core of our beings. It is not a
peripheral thing, a slight blemish that mars an otherwise
perfect specimen; sin is radical, touching the root of our
lives. This flies in the face of our cultural assumptions.
We grow up hearing that no one is good, but we take it
lightly and forget about sin. Yet Jesus said this about
human beings, 'A corrupt tree is bound to produce a
corrupt fruit.' He calls the people of his day 'an evil
generation.' The Nazi who marched people into the
death camp could go home to play with his children.
That is the reality. It was Jesus who said that from within
come evil thoughts, sexual immorality, theft, murder,
adultery, covetousness, wickedness, deceit, sensuality,
pride, etc. Jesus said there is none good but God. No one
but Jesus spoke with such clarity about humanity and its
total corruption and alienation from God. There seems to
be little evidence in the Bible that Jesus believed in
original goodness! Paul sums it up like this

> As it is written: 'There is no one righteous, not even one;
> there is no one who understands, no one who seeks God. All
> have turned away, they have together become worthless;
> there is no one who does good, not even one' (Rom. 3:10–12).

What does it mean to say that no one has done good? We
all know people that we would describe as good. The
issue is: who are we comparing them with? The standard

of goodness is God. Against that standard of goodness everything falls short. Wherever people are born, whatever their environment or upbringing, they fall short of the glory of God. In the great commandment, Jesus says this: 'Love the Lord your God with all your heart, all your heart, all your strength. And love your neighbour as you love yourself.' None of us loves God like that.

What are the implications of this radical corruption? For one thing, it means that it is impossible for humans to be objective, either in their arguments or in their scientific findings. There is no total objectivity anywhere. We strive to be objective in our reports and our scientific experiments, and sometimes we manage it. But even at our best moments our views are shot through with our own agenda. I say it for myself as a Christian preacher: I am to be constantly tested against the word I preach. Am I interpreting Scripture against Scripture or am I making it fit my agenda? We read our newspapers, turn on the television and listen to the news. And they don't just tell us what's happening; they tell us what's happening with a spin on what is happening. It happens in our Christian circles. Postmodernism dislikes the idea of objective truth, so some emergent church leaders suggest that we must ditch objective truth claims if we are going to reach this generation for Christ. Actually the reality is that both modernism and postmodernism have got it wrong and the Bible alone has it right.

I read books about people who are 'seekers.' It suggests that God is hiding and that people are out there looking for him. The Bible tells us that it is people who are hiding and deliberately looking in the wrong places. In the Garden of Eden, when humanity sinned and God came looking for Adam and Eve, who hid? Adam hid. Martin Luther observed that the pagan trembles at the rustling of a leaf. God's own take on the situation is that 'no one is righteous, not even one; there is no one who understands, no one who seeks God' (Rom. 3:10, 11). When God begins to draw someone to himself then that person will start to look for him, but the Scripture is saying that we humans do not by ourselves seek God.

The righteous judgement of God

God's righteous judgement comes in the context of his great patience, verse 3: 'The Lord said, "My Spirit will not contend with man for ever, for he is mortal; his days will be a hundred and twenty years."' In other words, God is saying 'My Spirit will not abide in man forever.' The life-giving Spirit is for God to give or recall. Is this inconsistent with God's love? What is the opposite of love? Everyone in a marriage will say that they will put up with most things except indifference. Indifference says, 'I don't care.' But God does care. Verse 6 says, 'The Lord was grieved that he had made man.' He loves the world, but he sees sin and it grieves him. He is holy and righteous and so he must punish sin. This response of God's is not the response of rage; it is God's slow, deliberate response to the evil he sees.

Open Theism, as we have seen, claims that God acts without a script, but that misses the point here: God is the unchanging God and he is pained by sin. Because he is unchanging, he will always change his plans to do people good if they resist his love. This is a strong reminder of the declaration that God is a God who carries out his threats as well as his promises. When he threatens, he means it. The descending of the flood was God's judicial response to universal sin. Jesus points to this event, and says that this is what is going to happen at the end of history.

As it was in the days of Noah, so it will be at the coming of the Son of Man. For in the days before the flood, people were eating and drinking, marrying and giving in marriage, up to the day Noah entered the ark; and they knew nothing about what would happen until the flood came and took them all away. That is how it will be at the coming of the Son of Man. Two men will be in the field; one will be taken and the other left. Two women will be grinding with a hand mill; one will be taken and the other left (Mt. 24:37–41).

Everyone is doing their own thing, eating, drinking and getting merry until Noah enters the ark. They refused to believe the warnings until the flood comes and takes them. Jesus is saying that judgement is an inevitable reality. It will bring eternal loss to those who reject the way of salvation. In 2 Peter, the apostle looks forward to a day much like today, when people do not take the idea of final judgement seriously.

They will say, 'Where is this "coming" he promised? Ever since our fathers died, everything goes on as it has since the beginning of creation.' But they deliberately forget that long ago by God's word the heavens existed and the earth was formed out of water and by water. By these waters also the world of that time was deluged and destroyed. By the same word the present heavens and earth are reserved for fire, being kept for the day of judgment and destruction of ungodly men (2 Pet. 3:4–7).

No wonder that the Bible said that when Noah built the ark, he did it in holy fear. That fear doesn't sit too well with us because we are rather familiar with God. This holy fear is a due sense of respect and awe of God's holiness. That's what Jesus is showing us in John 17 when he refers to his Father as Holy and Righteous Father. He is teaching us that we must have a holy respect for God. God is not tame. He is immensely powerful, utterly just and unbearably holy. It's folly if we find nothing to fear about God. Only toy lions are cuddly. But the real thing is very scary. An Old Testament prophet cried out about God: 'The Lion has roared.' This is our God.

The story of the flood reminds us that there is an end to grace. However unpopular such a message is, people need to hear it. Jesus never flinched from teaching that God had appointed a Day of Judgement and that he, Jesus himself, was going to be the Judge on that day. The reason why the word salvation (a rescue word) is used so often in the Bible is that there is something we need to be rescued from.

The only way of salvation

Verse 8: 'Noah found favour in the eyes of the Lord.' Or the word could be 'grace.' This is the first use of the word grace in the entire Bible. And it comes before there is any record of Noah's life. When that word is mentioned at the end of verse 8, Noah is standing where everyone is standing, under the judgement of God. Everyone is under the judgement, but Noah found grace. Or as Alec Motyer says, 'It's probably better to say that grace found Noah.'

There is a formula in the Hebrew here that is used several times in the Old Testament. It's used about Lot who was rescued from Sodom. He didn't deserve to be, but he was. It's used about a man who rejoiced in the name of Mephibosheth. King David shows kindness to him. Mephibosheth was Jonathan's son, and it was usual then to get rid of the last king's family in case they were a danger to you, but 'Mephibosheth found grace.' David showed grace to him. Wherever this phrase is used, it always focuses on someone receiving a kindness or mercy, who doesn't deserve it; and it has to do with saving someone. It means showing amazing grace or kindness or love to unworthy people, resulting in their salvation from great danger.

Grace made a difference in Noah's life. In verse 9 there is a break in the chapter, a natural division to the book of Genesis as Moses divides it all up by using an expression that stands on its own. In the Hebrew, it is 'This is the story of Noah', and it means 'generations of' or 'the account of' and it is like saying 'so far, so good.' Then he tells us what the effects of grace were: 'Noah was a righteous man, blameless among the people of his time, and he walked with God.' In verse 8 he is a meritless man and is shown grace. In verse 9 he is a righteous man. The thing that makes a difference is the grace of God. As it says in Ephesians 1:8–9, 'it is by grace you have been saved, through faith – and this not from yourselves, it is the gift of God – not by works, so that no one can boast. '

Grace saves us that so that we can perform good works. Grace found Noah and grace saved Noah. In his prayer Jesus calls his Father Righteous Father, and the righteousness of God is at work here. Many, many hundred and thousand of years later, the issues that were faced here were faced by the apostle Paul. How can God be righteous and save an unrighteous man like Noah? His grace is not like a helicopter that can just lift him up out of the coming wrath. Noah will have to go through the flood himself like the rest.

But God makes a covenant with Noah. This is the first time this word is used in the Bible though I introduced the idea when describing the relationship between God and Adam and Eve in the Garden of Eden. We know what a covenant is because, at a much lesser level, we enter into agreements when we buy freezers or dishwashers. There are two parties and there are promises to pay and promises of guarantee. A biblical covenant is shorthand for 'God's promise of salvation.' God says to this man, 'You are going to face judgement like everyone else. But I will act on your behalf. When the judgement falls, I will keep you safe.' And he does. Noah enters the ark with all the animals and is spared. God wraps him round with his promises and places him in this secure place so that, when the judgement falls, he will be safe. Locked up in that big dark tomb of an ark, Noah and his family were able to pass safely through the time of God's judgement.

In the New Testament Christ is our ark. The Apostle Peter uses this image

> For Christ died for sins once for all, the righteous for the unrighteous, to bring you to God. He was put to death in the body but made alive by the Spirit, through whom also he went and preached to the spirits in prison, who disobeyed long ago when God waited patiently in the days of Noah while the ark was being built. In it only a few people, eight in all, were saved through water, and this water symbolizes baptism that now saves you also – not the removal of dirt from the body but the pledge of a good conscience toward God. It saves you by the resurrection of Jesus Christ (1 Pet. 3:18–21).

When someone is in Christ, along with all the rest of the believing people of God, they are perfectly safe from judgement. The God who delivered Noah will deliver us and bring us to final salvation. That full and final salvation is sealed to us in Christian baptism, and we are sure of our salvation because of the resurrection of Christ.

Christ is our ark, for he is the only hope of salvation for the world. One of Paul's great descriptions of a Christian is of someone 'in Christ.' It is he 'who rescues us from the coming wrath' (1 Thess. 1:10). Noah is pointed to a rainbow as the covenant sign that God will never again judge the whole world by a flood: next time it will be by fire.

The animals are saved with Noah, just as through the fire of the final judgement this universe will be renewed, including the animal kingdom. One Sunday morning, I noticed outside our church window a pigeon being set upon by other pigeons. It was in obvious distress, and the others were attacking it mercilessly. It upset me to see it and I felt helpless. As I pondered it later, I remembered some words of John Calvin about the animals, 'They are as they are because we are what we are.' We have brought all of nature down with us in our fall. But the Christian knows something else. Just as the animals were saved because of Noah's faith, so all creation is waiting 'in eager expectation for the sons of God to be revealed' (Rom. 8:19). On that day the 'the creation itself (both nature and animals) will be liberated from its bondage to decay and brought into the glorious freedom of the children of God' (Rom. 8:21).

We are living today not pre-Flood but pre-Fire. As in Noah's day, there is coming a time when God will shut the door and all who are outside of Christ will be shut up to wrath. This is the tough but true message of Jesus himself. It was Jesus who quoted the days of Noah and compared them with the final judgement to come. It was Jesus who told parables that described the exclusion of those who were not prepared for the wedding feast. If we are going to be honest with people we have to leave this solemn truth in the message we preach alongside the equally important truth that today is a day of salvation.

Today the door is open. Jesus says 'I am the door' and he invites people through us to come to him to find life. So the days of Noah leave us with a further insight into the human problem. Who is going to resolve the issue of sin, who will rescue us from coming wrath? Where can people find safety when the judgement of God falls?

Act 1 Scene 4

Generation eXodus

We're coming up to the climax of Act 1 – the Passover, that moment when God saves his people from the tyranny and slavery of Egypt, and delivers them out of Pharaoh's hand. At this moment of high drama, what is significant to our story is the death of the firstborn and the place of blood in the rescue and release of God's people.

Recently I was preaching in Germany and the conference where I was speaking was held in a former Hitler youth camp, built around 1933. I was impressed with the building and with the facilities provided back then. It must have been state of the art for the 1930s, and have made an enormous impression on the young people who went. And as I stood in the lecture room teaching the Bible, I couldn't help but think of these young people sitting in the same room listening to Nazi propaganda long ago. Then I discovered that in fact children and young people from that very camp had been shipped out to the Russian front and sacrificed there on the altar of a false ideology, for one of the most brutal regimes in history.

The world has had more than its fair share of tyranny. Hitler and Stalin are two modern examples, but the Pharaoh of Egypt, who is in this story in Exodus, would certainly have qualified to join the club. He used slave labour for his great building projects, such as the Pyramids. But bad though Pharaoh undoubtedly was, we would be very wrong if we thought of the story of the Exodus as merely a story about political liberty, for it is not.

The transfiguration

The early Christians regarded the Old Testament as a Christian book; it was their Scriptures before they had the New Testament. At the end of Luke's gospel, after the resurrection, we find Jesus explaining why it was necessary that the Messiah should suffer and then enter into his glory: 'beginning with Moses and all the prophets, he interpreted to them in all the Scriptures the things concerning himself' (Lk. 24:27).

In Luke chapter 9, there is that crucial moment when Jesus starts out for Jerusalem with the cross on his mind. The incident took place on a mountain. Jesus had been busy for many days, healing, teaching, and he had taken his three closest friends with him: Peter, James and John, and they had gone onto the mountain to pray.

As Jesus was praying, the disciples fell asleep. Luke tells us that when they awoke, they were amazed to find Jesus transfigured before them. The word 'transfigured' or 'transfiguration' is the Greek word 'metamorphosed.' He had changed in his appearance, and it was as if his whole body was translucent with light, with the glory of God shining out through the thin veil of his humanity. And they saw two others, Moses and Elijah, with Jesus on the mountain. Luke tells us in 9:31 that the three of them were having a conversation about Jesus' coming 'departure which he was to accomplish at Jerusalem.'

They were talking, obviously, about Jesus' death. But the interesting thing is that the word 'departure' used by Luke is the Greek word 'exodus'. There is a deliberate link with the Old Testament story; the death of Jesus in Jerusalem would mark the moment when a greater liberation and Exodus was going to be accomplished than had occurred under Moses in the original Exodus. Luke is saying that Jesus' death was going to be an act of salvation for the world, far more significant than the Exodus in the past. And, in particular, the death of Jesus was going to be an echo of an event in Exodus 12 – the Passover.

What was the background? The children of Israel have been in Egypt for four hundred years and, as time has passed, their lot has become more difficult. By this point, they are slaves, charged with the backbreaking work of building the Pyramids and other great structures. Here are people who had a promise that Abraham had given to them, and some still clung to it: others despaired. We are told earlier in Exodus that they had begun to cry out because of their bondage. Some had called upon God, and others were simply calling out in complaint because of their experiences.

The burning bush

A number of years before, Moses had been saved from death as a child and then, having made an abortive attempt to become the rescuer of his people, had had to leave Egypt as fast as he could for his life. Whilst he was out in the desert, he had an encounter with God (Ex. 3).

There he heard the word of God, and in that word that God gave him, over forty years before the time of Exodus 12, God had told him what he was going to do. God said, 'You've got to go back to Egypt. You've got to confront the king of Egypt, Pharaoh. You've got to tell him to let my people go. He won't listen to you, but you've got to tell him to let my people go. And I want you to perform signs and wonders that demonstrate that I am God in Egypt, and he will still not let the people go. And eventually I'm going to have to kill the firstborn.' So the word of God preceded the events described in the rest of Exodus. Alec Motyer puts it like this: 'Moses was a man who was wise before the event.'[10]

God told Moses certain things. First of all he said that he was the God of Moses' fathers: Abraham, Isaac and Jacob, the God of the Patriarchs, the covenant God who had made promises in the past, and now intended to keep these promises. Secondly, he revealed himself to Moses as the God of holiness. In the Bible, that burning bush marks the first time that we are introduced to this idea of the holiness of God: it has only been hinted at before. It is a necessary preparation for our understanding about what is going on at the Exodus.

Thirdly, God told Moses that his purpose was to save his people from captivity. God said, 'I have come down to deliver them out of the hands of the Egyptians.' Then God tells Moses that Israel is God's adopted son, his firstborn. It is all summed up in Exodus 6:6 when God says to Moses, 'I am the Lord and I will bring you out from under the yoke of the Egyptians. I will free you from being slaves to them, and I will redeem you with an outstretched arm and with mighty acts of judgement.' What did Moses know before he went back to Egypt? He knew that God had adopted his people, that God had committed himself to redeem them, to break the power of

Egypt and to bring them out of bondage into the Promised Land.

The action moves on – to Egypt and the huge show-down that is at the very heart of Exodus 12. The drama moves to God revealing himself in Egypt, concerned to demonstrate that he and he alone is God. We are still looking at this through the lens of Jesus' prayer in John 17, and in that prayer, Jesus defines what people need to believe in order to become Christians. He says in verse 3, 'This is eternal life that they may know you, the only true God, and Jesus Christ whom you have sent.' One of Moses' great tasks was to demonstrate to Pharaoh and all of Egypt that the Lord God of Israel was the only true God.

Jesus said this about his own life and ministry: 'I have revealed you to those whom you gave me out of the world' (Jn. 17:6). Moses had done the same – manifested God's name to the people in his day. And in John 17 Jesus is talking like another Moses, whose great job was to tell Israel God's name. Who is the only true God? This was one of the questions being posed and answered by the showdown with Pharaoh. The signs and wonders performed in Egypt identified the God of Israel as the Lord of creation, just as the signs and wonders Jesus performed demonstrated that he was God's Messiah. He is in a position to tell us who God is.

The wrath of God

God uses two words to describe these plagues. They are blows and they are signs. They are intended to be both acts of judgement and signs that teach us something about the nature and character of God.

What do they point to? Firstly, they point to the wrath of God. Some theologians want us to believe that God is a

God of love only. But the Bible will not let us have such a whittled down shadow of a God. In these Old Testament pictures that Jesus authenticates, we discover that the plagues are acts of judgement. God says in chapter 12:12: 'I will pass through Egypt and strike down every firstborn – both men and animals – and I will bring judgement on all the gods of Egypt. I am the LORD.'

Here is judgement against *Egypt's gods*. The Nile god Hapi was venerated as one of the chief gods of the land and so the first strike is against the Nile as it turns to blood. Heq was the frog-headed goddess of fruitfulness. Kepher took the form of a beetle. Many gods were depicted as animals. Nut was the sky goddess. Seraphia was the protector against the locusts. The ninth plague strikes out against the second major god, Ra, the sun god. There is a terrible darkness on the land. You cannot read about this terrible darkness without recalling that, as Jesus hung on the cross, there was period of three hours when the sun was obscured and an awful darkness came across the land. God has always hated idolatry and he still does.

Here also is judgement against *Egypt's wickedness*. And it is right here that we find ourselves most at odds with our society. It is also here that many of our friends stumble. Why should God send such revolting and harmful plagues upon these people? Surely there can be no justification for this? They may well complain that this is a God they want nothing to do with.

It is a sheer fact of human history that one of the first doctrines of God to be jettisoned by people anxious to get away from him is the doctrine of judgement. But the Bible will not let us back off from the truth of the wrath of God against sin and the judgement of God against sinners. There is a distinctly penal element to this action of God. God is a God of blinding holiness. His word rules the universe. To sin against such a God is to expose ourselves to infinite repercussions. J. A. Motyer has said

> We have a problem with the plagues simply because we step back from the truth of the wrath of God against sin and the judgement of God upon sinners. We would prefer the bliss of a kingdom of God without moral absolutes, presided over by a God without wrath and entered through a Christ without a cross. But the price for this would be to discard not just this or that bit of the Bible but the whole God-given book, for in it God has revealed his absolutes and that he is a God of intense, fiery holiness. Jesus died bearing our sins in his body on the cross, for that is what sin merits, and saving us from the wrath to come, for that is where sin leads.[11]

It is impossible to escape the clear teaching of the text that the plagues on Egypt were part of the retributive judgement of God. God hates disobedience every bit as much as he loves obedience. The day is coming when Jesus Christ will break into human history, stop the human story as we know it, raise the dead and then pronounce judgement on them. Jesus was unequivocal about this

> For as the Father has life in himself, so he has granted the Son to have life in himself. And he has given him authority to judge because he is the Son of Man.
> Do not be amazed at this, for a time is coming when all who are in their graves will hear his voice and come out – those who have done good will rise to live, and those who have done evil will rise to be condemned (Jn. 5:26–29).

The tenth plague is definitive. It has an elaborate introduction given to it in chapter 11:1–10. It stands out in contrast to all the other plagues. God was involved with them, of course, using Moses as his instrument. But now God acts himself to work his just judgement. 'If the plagues begin with the disasters sin brings, they lead inexorably to the death with which sin ends.'[12] As the apostle Paul teaches us, 'the wages of sin is death' (Rom. 6:23). That this is the most important and definitive plague is obvious from the fact that this is God's stated intention. This is where everything has been headed. The delay has been a gracious delay, but the end has been fixed.

The mercy of God

These plagues are also mixed with God's mercy. In chapters 3 and 4, God had said to Moses that Pharaoh is not going to let them go and that he is going to have to bring death in the end. So why then did God put Moses through this process of sending plague after plague after plague? The answer is that God is slow to anger. Whenever he judges he mixes it with mercy. That's why in the book of Revelation, when John is talking about the end of history, he describes the trumpet judgements, and then eventually the bowls of wrath that mark the final judgement, but in between there are these unexpected events that happen, that make us think, that are meant to say to the world, 'Repent, get ready. Get right with God, and do it now.'

In the process of these plagues, many Egyptians saw the evidence of God's work and joined themselves to the covenant people. So quite a sizeable mixed multitude left Egypt. But others, including Pharaoh himself, refused to read the writing on the wall. Noah preached for 120 years and warned people about the flood, but they refused to believe. But the end came. We preach about final judgement coming and every day it doesn't is another opportunity for repentance. But the day will come. Are we to be silent about this? Are we to pretend that this isn't in the Bible? Are we to tell people that everything will be all right, when it most decidedly will not? These are issues we face in our preaching and witness today. To be silent would betray a whole generation of people and leave their blood on our hands. Evangelical leaders who talk as if this were a matter of mere debate within the evangelical family are playing with fire. God in his patience will wait and wait and wait, but the end will come.

The real issue of the plagues is this: unsheltered humanity cannot stand in the presence of God the Judge. Those who deny the existence of sin seem to be ignoring death. Sin is a capital offence. It leads to death. And sin is the evidence of our race's rebellion. Death is the sacrament of sin. It is the outward visible sign that whoever sins will die. We are under the judgement of God.

The lamb of God

The Passover teaches us that the Israelites were just as sinful as the Egyptians. We miss the point if we don't realise this. They would die too. God made sure that none of the preceding plagues went near the Israelites. But now God says that he is going to visit every home in Egypt – that means Israelite homes too. The soul that sins deserved to die. And it wasn't just the Egyptians that did not heed God's word. At the beginning of the book of Exodus, the Israelites didn't obey Moses. In fact they were going to continue to disobey. And the Israelites in Egypt had become worshippers of idols: Joshua 24:14

says, 'Throw away the gods your forefathers worshipped beyond the river of Egypt and serve the Lord.'

Everyone in the land of Egypt was ripe to experience the wrath of God unless God should make some provision for them to escape. And just as God had provided an ark to save Noah from his judgement of the earth, so God provided a lamb to save Israel from the judgement of Egypt. On the night when the LORD went through the land of Egypt something died in every house, either the firstborn died or the lamb died. The New Testament gives us an explicit explanation of what this signifies for us. In 1 Corinthians 5:7 we read, 'Christ, our Passover lamb, has been sacrificed.'

Selection

The Israelites were told to take great care on the selection of the lamb (Ex. 12: 5–6). The lamb 'must be year-old males without defect, and you may take them from the sheep or the goat. Take care of them until the fourteenth day of the month, when all the people of the community of Israel must slaughter them at twilight.' This was to be enshrined in the Israelites' code of practice from that time onwards. Any sacrifice that was given to God had to be spotless, without a flaw or blemish.

Moses warned the people not to bring anything with a defect because it wouldn't be accepted on their behalf. At the end of the Old Testament, God complains through Malachi that the people were bringing to him defective animals that were unworthy of him and unacceptable to him. They merely brought a curse back on those who offered them to him. The sacrifice had to be perfect.

In the New Testament there is much made about the perfection of our Lord Jesus. An imperfect person will die for their own sins. But only the sinless One can die for the sins of others. Jesus is our Lamb: the apostle Peter tells us in 1 Peter 1:19, we were redeemed with 'the precious blood of Christ, a lamb without blemish or defect.'

Substitution

Great care was also to be taken on the substitution of the lamb. Verse 3 and following shows the care with which they chose the lamb

> Tell the whole community of Israel that on the tenth day of this month each man is to take a lamb for his family, one for each household. If any household is too small for a whole lamb, they must share one with their nearest neighbour, having taken into account the number of people there are. You are to determine the amount of lamb needed in accordance with what each person will eat (Ex.12:3–4).

There has to be enough lamb for the right number of people. And if anything is left over, it has to be burned the next day because it has accomplished its goal. The whole point of this care is to emphasise the substitution aspect. The lamb was instead of the people.

In 12:30 we read this: 'There was not a house in Egypt without someone dead.' The lamb had died for God's firstborn, Israel. It has always been God's way to provide what he demands. There is a background to this story. Earlier in their history, Abraham had taken his son Isaac up to a mountain to sacrifice him to the Lord. He went in faith believing that God would provide a lamb. And at the last moment God did just that (Gen. 22:7–13). There was still this memory among the people of God. The Lord will provide a lamb.

Philip Graham Ryken very helpfully explains the progression of the Bible with respect of the lamb:

At first God provided one lamb for one person. Thus Abraham offered a ram in place of his son Isaac. Next God provided one lamb for one household. This happened at the first Passover, when every family in the covenant community offered its own lamb to God. Then God provided one sacrifice for the whole nation. On the Day of Atonement, a single animal atoned for the sins of all Israel. Finally the day came when John the Baptist 'saw Jesus coming toward him and said, "Look, the lamb of God, who takes away the sin of the world!"' (Jn.1:29). God was planning this all along: one lamb to die for one world. By his grace he has provided a lamb – 'the lamb that was slain from the creation of the world' (Rev.13:8).[13]

Twice in John's gospel, Jesus is identified as 'the lamb of God who takes away the sin of the world.'

The salvation of God

What was it that made the difference that night when the Holy Lord visited Egypt? When they were making the film *Prince of Egypt*, the makers wanted to add God saying something like this, 'When I see the mark I will pass over you.' But all the religious advisers, both Jewish and Christian, who were helping them said, 'No, you can't say that.' It says in verse 13 quite clearly 'The blood will be a sign for you on the houses where you are; and when I see the blood, I will pass over you.'

Salvation is through faith

These people had to do what God said. Every action had to be driven by the fact that God was going to act. They were told to hide under the covering of the blood, and that was what they did. They killed the lambs, they sprinkled the blood on the doorposts of their houses in an act of faith. That's how we become Christians; we take God at his word. This is what God says: 'Believe in the Lord Jesus and you will be saved.' Salvation comes through faith in the blood of the lamb.

Salvation comes by blood

The Lord says, 'when I see the blood, I will pass over you.' The God of judgement, who came to impose a penalty of death justly due, saw the blood and passed over in peace. It is the blood which solves the problem of acceptance before God. The people who have taken shelter in the blood-marked houses discover they are safe from the fearful judgement that falls all around them. Many Egyptians also listened to what Moses said, believed it and found refuge in the home of the Israelites. So when the Israelites left Egypt they left with a mixed multitude of people who had believed the word of God.

The shed blood had a double value of satisfying God and keeping the people secure. The technical words for these two aspects are expiation and propitiation. Expiation means 'to cover.' The people who sheltered under the blood were already saved. Propitiation means to 'turn away wrath,' to 'divert judgement.' When the Lord came bringing God's judgement to Egypt, he saw the blood on the doorposts and he 'passed over' those homes. Wrath was averted and judgement was carried out on an innocent other.

Notice the language God uses. He is satisfied when he sees the blood. The blood makes the difference. Why? Because it represents life taken violently. Sin is a capital offence and the blood indicates that the price is paid. The blood was a sign to the Israelites that a substitute had died in their place (Ex. 12:13). When I was a boy, I realised what this meant as I was reading this story. I, too, was a firstborn son. And I loved to see lambs playing in the fields near our home. I imagined what it must have been like for the firstborn sons of Israel, children like me getting to keep a lamb in the house for four days before the night God had appointed. I knew I'd get attached to it and that I would be heartbroken when eventually it was slaughtered. And I imagined what my father would have said to me, 'Son, either the lamb dies or you die.' That takes us to the heart of it. God gave up his own Son, the lamb of God to die, so that I might never die eternal death but have eternal life.

It will not do to talk about Jesus substituting himself for us in 'some vague sort of way we can't define.' The text of the Passover event and the teaching about Jesus' death makes it perfectly clear that his death 'covered' the people and kept them safe by 'turning away the wrath and judgement' that was coming upon them. No wonder the New Testament writers are so full of this: 'We have been justified by his blood.' And 'In him we have redemption through his blood, the forgiveness of sins' (Rom. 5:9; Eph. 1:7).

We began this chapter with a reference to Jesus' prayer on the evening of his arrest. It was Passover, and we know that feast and its significance were on his mind. John 17 is the conclusion of a sustained teaching section which begins in the Upper Room. As the evening begins everything is placed in context. 'It was just before the Passover Feast. Jesus knew that the time had come for him to leave this world and go to the Father. Having loved his own who were in the world, he now showed them the full extent of his love' (Jn. 13:1). The next day as he hung on his cross dying for the sins of the world, it was at the same time as the lambs were being slain inside the Temple in memory of that first Passover. No wonder one of the most precious symbols of our Lord Jesus has been that of the lamb. This is how the apostle John delights to describe him in the book of Revelation. It is a 'lamb, looking as if it had been slain'(Rev. 5:6) who is the Lion of Judah, the rightful king who now takes his seat on the throne of God. The only hope for people is to have our names written 'before the foundation of the world in the book of life of the lamb that was slain' (Rev. 13:8 ESV). And John describes the end of history in these stark terms: people hiding themselves and 'calling on the mountains and rocks, "Fall on us and hide us from the face of him who is seated on the throne, and from the wrath of the lamb, for the great day of their wrath has come, and who can stand?"'(Rev. 6:16–17 ESV).

We started with the conversation between Moses, Elijah and Jesus on the Mount of Transfiguration. What becomes apparent is that the Passover was not simply a good illustration of what Jesus was about to do in Jerusalem. Rather, the sacrifice of the Messiah to save all who believe from the coming wrath of God and domination of Satan had been decided upon ages before. It was part of that eternal plan of redemption formed before the world existed, the first act in the drama.

When the Israelites got ready to leave Egypt that night they ate a meal together. That Passover meal has its Christian counterpart in the Lord's Supper. When we meet for that meal we are saying to the world that we are sustained by the work of the lamb for us. Just as the Israelites fed on the flesh of the slain lamb back then, so we feed on Christ in our hearts by faith.

Act 1 Scene 5

Yom Kippur

We live in an age of tolerance, or at least we think we do. Certainly we seem to be willing to tolerate the murderer, giving him about ten years or so for taking human life. We tolerate the murder of the unborn as if they were simply bits of tissue; we tolerate the most brazen plays of sexual dissoluteness in our media. We like to think that we are tolerant. We tolerate different views, especially views that contradict each other. What we cannot stomach, apparently, is intolerance. Of course we are intolerant of some things. We cannot stand paedophiles, people who hurt children or old ladies. We stand in judgement, through the tabloids, on the rich and famous who cheat on their wives, their employers or the taxman. And we cannot tolerate anyone else imposing on us their notion of moral or spiritual absolutes.

One of our pet hates is gratuitous violence. And we certainly cannot bear to think of a religion that encourages or suggests the use of violence in any shape or form. Some of us can remember the outrage that erupted on the pages of our newspapers when Mel Gibson's film *The*

Passion was about to be released. You would have imagined that what he was doing was encouraging mob violence, that releasing a film about the sufferings of one man was going to be the end of civilisation as we know it. Blood-sacrifice may have been a fact of life in the ancient world but it means absolutely nothing to people today except as a source of repugnance. In our next scene we move to look at one of the main events in the Old Testament which explains the significance of sacrifice.

As the curtain rises, the stage is set for the Day of Atonement and the world of Leviticus. Once again, we are watching an event that was on Jesus' mind as he prayed in John 17. The Day of Atonement – Yom Kippur as the Jews call it – is as much an antecedent of the Christian message as that other great event Jesus was thinking of, the Passover.

We know this to be the case for several reasons. In John 17, the prayer is divided into three: Jesus prays for himself (vs 1–5), for his disciples (vs 6–19) and for all believers in all places at all times (vs 20–26). And at the end of Leviticus 16, the high priest makes atonement for himself, his fellow priests and all the house of Israel. It was also the work of the high priest to consecrate the sacrificial victim on the altar. In John 17:19, Jesus uses these same words as he anticipates going to the cross: 'And for their sakes I consecrate myself' (ESV). That is to say, 'I set myself apart for holy service to God.' In the case of Christ, he is both the offerer and the offering. Later, the writer of Hebrews makes this connection explicit in his description of Jesus, our great high priest. Hebrews 9:14 says, 'Christ offered himself unblemished to God.' And twice in John's Gospel someone says: 'Behold the lamb of God who takes the sin of the world,' conflating together the Passover and the Day of Atonement.

The Day of Atonement was the most solemn day in the Jewish religious calendar. The New Testament regards the Old Testament as God's picturebook and Christ's textbook. In all his dealings with these people, God is setting up precedents of behaviour and action that give us understanding of the even greater mystery of his Son's coming into the world. We really cannot understand what Christ is doing until we understand something of the Old Testament teaching.

What are the elements of the drama described in Leviticus 16? The book of Exodus ends with God coming to live in the midst of his people. That must have excited them. They had been given detailed instructions for the framing of the tabernacle; every detail had been carefully spelled out. This tent in the middle of the camp was to be the visible tangible focus of God's promises to these people and God's presence with them.

> So I will consecrate the Tent of Meeting and the altar and will consecrate Aaron and his sons to serve me as priests. Then I will dwell among the Israelites and be their God. They will know that I am the LORD their God, who brought them out of Egypt so that I might dwell among them. I am the LORD their God (Ex. 29:44–46).

This was the climax of redemption; God had brought them out of Egypt so he could be with them.

Once it was made, the great day came. It must have been a heart-stopping occasion. Here was God's tent being erected among their tents. God was coming to take up residence. 'Then the cloud covered the Tent of Meeting, and the glory of the LORD filled the tabernacle.' But 'Moses *could not enter* the Tent of Meeting because the cloud had settled upon it, and the glory of the LORD filled the tabernacle' (Ex. 40:34–35). 'God is present but is not available; he is next door but not a neighbour.'[14]

What is the problem? God is Holy. And the book of Leviticus is about how that problem is resolved. How do unholy people visit God in his home, the tabernacle?

Leviticus 1 is the transition point. The Lord called to Moses from the Tent of Meeting, He said, 'Speak to the Israelites and say to them whenever any of you bring an offering to the LORD . . .' They can visit God in his home and bring an offering. Literally, the Hebrew reads: the offering is what brings you near. The sacrifices unite us to God. The people cannot enter into God's house but they can draw near on the basis of sacrifice.

The presenting problem

This chapter begins with a warning. 'The LORD spoke to Moses after the death of the two sons of Aaron who died when they approached the LORD' (Lev. 16:1). Back in chapter 10 two men had died because they didn't take the holiness of God seriously. 'Aaron's sons Nadab and Abihu took their censers, put fire in them and added incense; and they offered unauthorized fire before the LORD, contrary to his command. So fire came out from the presence of the LORD and consumed them, and they died before the LORD.' The whole structure of this religious way may mean little to us but to the people then it was God saying to them, 'Approach me with caution.' Why?

God is Holy

The whole first section of this book deals with the problem of human defilement and estrangement from God. We are separated from God. This was visually demonstrated in the layout of the tabernacle, the worship centre of ancient Israel. At the heart of the tabernacle was a small room. It was separated from the rest of the structure by a thickly woven curtain. Behind this curtain, in this room called The Holy Place, was an oblong box called the Ark of the Covenant. In this box were placed a copy of the Ten Commandments and the rod used by Moses in Egypt when he performed the signs of God's power and some manna which sustained the people in the desert. But the important thing for us is that the top of the box had two massive cherubim figures with their wings bending inwards over the flat centre of the top of the box. That space was called the Mercy Seat; it was the symbolic throne of God. I say 'symbolic' for the God of Israel could no more be confined to a room inside a tent than he could be captured like a genie in a bottle. The universe is too small for him. He fills all things. But this was the place which he chose to designate as his earthly throne, the place where he met with his people.

The tabernacle symbolised the presence of God right at the centre of the nation's life. It stressed that it was no light thing to be in the presence of God. Hence the warning about a couple of priests who acted out of order and the detailed instructions on how the high priest was to dress, wash and prepare himself to approach God. Everything was carefully laid out to emphasise the holiness of God: to come into God's presence there had to be cleanliness.

Why couldn't people just go into God's throne room any way they wanted? The clue was what was in the box. In the box were the Ten Commandments. The Ten Commandments were given for at least two reasons. Firstly, they were a description of what God is like. This is his character, this is the kind of person that he is. But the Ten Commandments were also given as a mirror to hold up to ourselves.

Alec Motyer comments: 'there are two images of God on earth. There is the image of God in humanity and there is the image of God in the law of God.'[15] The biblical deduction from that is that if we are to manifest the image of God as human beings, then we need to live a normal life, and we must pattern that life on the Law of God because the law is a verbal statement of what God is like. 'The law is what it is because God is as he is.' As it is, the Law exposes us as sinners.

What can be done about sin?

Sin is pervasive and contagious. It must be dealt with, for it kills, it leads to death. And it is a complex problem. This chapter uses four words to describe how our sin offends our Holy God.

In verse 16 it is called *uncleanness*. Our behaviour so pollutes the world we live in that we have made it uninhabitable for God. He is uncomfortable among us. He cannot bear to live with us. Sin pollutes us and keeps God away from us. So sin needs to be cleansed, and there is an elaborate ritual involved. The very Holy Place itself has to be cleansed and the agent God has chosen is blood. Everything has to be sprinkled 'seven times to cleanse it and to consecrate it from the uncleanness of the Israelites' (Lev. 16:19).

Sin is also *transgression* (Lev. 16:16 ESV). This word is also translated *rebellion*. It is an essentially legal offence. It describes what people do when they deliberately go against God's will, revealed in God's law. The law we break is the law of God, who sustains us from day to day, who gives us life and breath and our very existence. He is the one who has come to us in love in Christ. All relationships have boundaries, even the closest ones. This is much truer of our relationship with the Holy God. To

transgress those boundaries, to break those laws, is to
alienate ourselves from him and to incur his judicial
wrath. This involves incurring penalties, in particular
death.

Sin is *wickedness* or *iniquity*.[16] Sin is *sin* (Lev. 16;16, 21,
30, 34). This is a catch-all word that covers everything we
do that is wrong, 'serious or trivial, deliberate or
unintentional, conscious or unconscious, visible or
invisible, an act of disposition, consisting of commission
or of omission.'[17]

We discover here Israel's problem and the universal
problem. 'All have sinned and fall short of the glory of
God.' We are all stuck on the outside; kept at a distance
from the presence of God; unable and unworthy even to
try to gain access on our own terms. What do we need?
We need radical cleansing for our uncleanness, an end to
our wilful disobedience, a pardon for our rebellion and
forgiveness for our sin. Only the offended One himself
can prescribe the way back to himself. Nor will this come
cheaply. It will cost something. And it will require God to
show us the way back to him.

We mustn't think that this is just Old Testament
teaching and that somehow it is inferior to the teaching of
the New Testament. Our Lord Jesus himself was shaped
by the teaching of the Old Testament. He put his seal of
approval on it. And when he called his Father 'Holy and
Righteous', his idea of what holiness meant was entirely
drawn from this Old Testament description. We only
understand the Day of Atonement and the death of Jesus
when we understand that God is majestic in his holiness
and that this Holy God has been offended by his
creatures in many ways. There is a mountain of
uncleanness to climb and humanity simply cannot climb
it.

The mediating priest

The Day of Atonement was to be a Sabbath of Sabbaths. This means it was a day when absolutely no-one was to do any kind of work. Except the high priest, that is. He comes as a sinner. He can't come any way he chooses or he'll die. There is no one more authorised than the high priest to go in there and to worship within that holy place, and yet he dare not got unprepared. He must go through the process of washing and clothing before he can enter. He has to offer a bull for his own sins before he can deal with the sin of others. And he is to burn incense so that the holy place is full of smoke, so that he cannot see the presence of God, because no one can see the presence of God and stay alive.

The New Testament picks up the very fact that the high priest was a sinner who had to offer a sacrifice for himself. Hebrews 7 tells us that our great high priest, in contrast, is without sin

> Unlike the other high priests, he does not need to offer sacrifices day after day, first for his own sins, and then for the sins of the people. He sacrificed for their sins once for all when he offered himself. For the law appoints as high priests men who are weak; but the oath, which came after the law, appointed the Son, who has been made perfect forever (Heb. 7:27–28).

The mediating priest also comes as a servant. Exodus stipulates that the high priest had to wear a whole host of ornamental robes and head dress – but not today. On this day he has to dress in a simple white linen robe. And verse 17 says he has to be absolutely alone, for he alone can work on this day. So Christ came as a servant and was entirely alone when he offered himself up to atone for the sins of the world:

> From the sixth hour until the ninth hour darkness came over
> all the land. About the ninth hour Jesus cried out in a loud
> voice, *'Eloi, Eloi, lama sabachthani?'* – which means, 'My God,
> my God, why have you forsaken me?'* (Mt. 27:46).

What drama this involved! The whole nation gathered to
watch one simply dressed individual, as he goes into the
Holy of Holies. The question in everybody's mind would
be 'Will he come out alive?' They even tied a cord to his
ankle just in case he should be overwhelmed by God's
presence or consumed by God's holiness. If that were to
happen, they could then pull him out! There would be
great suspense – and then great relief (v18) when he came
out and everyone knew the sacrifices had been accepted.

The atoning provision

In a carefully orchestrated drama, two animals are taken
to represent one atoning provision. What happens out of
sight, behind the curtain, is demonstrated for all to see by
the action in public before the eyes of all Israel. The high
priest has to take two goats, one to be slaughtered and
the other to be released into the wilderness.

The sin-offering – the goat that is slain

The goat selected for sacrifice is to be slaughtered, its
blood shed and then taken into the Holy Place and
sprinkled on the mercy seat. The laying on of hands is a
signal of the   transference of guilt and sin. Sin is
transferred to the first animal and it is killed in the
sinners' place. Blood represents life; and shed blood
represents life violently taken. The 'blood' is evidence of
physical death. And a sacrifice can be made in

atonement. Instead of the death of his people, God has appointed the death of a substitute. This is a crucial point. There is a life given in exchange for a life, an innocent life surrendered on behalf of a guilty life.

The scapegoat – the goat that is sent

After the sacrifice, the high priest is to take the live goat. He has to confess all the sins on the goat's head. The goat is to be taken to a solitary place and released. What happened inside the holy place was secret. What happened to the scapegoat was entirely public. It was the disappearance of the scapegoat that reassured the people of their pardon.

When we look at the New Testament we find Jesus fulfilling both these images. He enters the presence of God by offering himself as a sacrifice for our sins. On the cross he is acting in our place, bearing the penalty of sin (this is called penal substitution). His sacrifice achieves the removal of our sin. Then Jesus cries out on the cross: 'My God, my God, why have you forsaken me?' Where is Jesus going as he goes into the darkness on that cross? He is going to that place of abandonment. He has become the scapegoat. He is the Lamb of God, the Passover lamb. He has taken the sin of the people on himself. Leviticus 16 is being fulfilled. As Jesus hangs on the cross, the curtain that hides the holy place from the eyes of the priest and everyone else, is torn from top to bottom, as God announces that the one high priest has made the one effective offering for all time. Hebrews 10 says, 'Therefore, brothers, since we have confidence to enter the Most Holy Place by the blood of Jesus . . .' No wonder Satan hates this. This deals with the problem of sin.

On one occasion Napoleon Bonaparte, with his staff officers around him and a big map of the world spread out before him, put his finger on the map on a little kingdom coloured red and said, 'Monsieurs, if it were not for that red spot, I could conquer the world.' That little spot was the British Isles. That's Satan's problem. He puts his finger on Calvary where Jesus died and he can say to his cohorts, 'If it were not for that little red spot, I could conquer the world.' No wonder Satan hates the cross.

On the Day of Atonement no one worked but the high priest. Today the only way to salvation is to accept the work of our great high priest. There is no work for us to do to get salvation. It's all been done and we must rest in what Jesus has done for us, if we are to know that we have access into the throne room of God. The message of the gospel is simply this: God is holy but he loves us.

Act 2 Scene 1

The scandal of forgiveness

A London psychiatrist once told Dr Billy Graham that 70 per cent of the people in treatment in England could be released if they could find forgiveness. Their problem, he said, was guilt, and they could gain no relief from the grief and pressure under which they lived.

Often people today are told they have nothing to be guilty about, and in some circumstances that is true. Some people feel guilty about things they have not done: things that have been done to them by responsible adults, who have abused or misused them. They need help to see who is to blame. But most people with guilty consciences don't need to be told that they are guiltless. Deep down they know there is something to be guilty for, and what they need is not to be told that they are guiltless, but that they are forgiven.

David's guilt

Certainly that's what King David needed. As the curtain rises on this scene, Psalm 51, we can see a miserable figure on the stage. David is suffering. His bones are

69

crushed. He feels the way you feel when you've had long, sleepless nights, tossing to and fro on your bed. You can get no rest from something that is torturing your mind. David knew that pressure, that physical pressure of guilt weighing down on him and crushing him.

The problem wasn't that he *felt* guilty; it was that he *was* guilty. David is guilty of the double sin of adultery and murder. Here is a man who has walked with God for many years. He is described in the Bible as a man after God's own heart and the sweet singer of Israel. He has gained a reputation as a prophet: someone who understood the deep things of God, and he is established as a spiritual as well as national leader of his people. But then he plunges into this terrible double sin.

It was quite a straightforward story. In his success and affluence, David had been lounging around when he ought to have been at war with his soldiers. And as he was doing so, he noted the pretty wife of a petty courtier. He wasn't content merely to lust from a distance, and it wasn't long before the lady in question sent him a note to tell him that she was now pregnant with his child. Now what? He is the King. If he made the wrong choice, it could destabilise his kingdom.

David came up with a plan. He would recall the woman's husband, Uriah, from war, in the hope that he would sleep with his wife and think that the child was his. What David didn't consider was that Uriah was a man of integrity. He had a problem enjoying himself while his comrades were still away fighting. He loved the King and his country and felt that he had to deny himself the normal pleasures of a married man. So he didn't sleep with his wife. The King tried to get him drunk, hoping that he would change his mind. He didn't.

Uriah goes back to the front line and David decides that the only way out is to get rid of him. And he arranges that when the soldiers are on a dangerous manoeuvre, Uriah should be cut off from the rest of the army and left to take the consequences. Uriah dies on the battlefield, David marries the woman, and everything seems to be sorted. No-one knows, apart from him and Bathsheba, and David thinks he has got away with it – until Nathan the prophet comes to see him. He tells David a story of gross injustice, and then tells David –'You are the man.' This Psalm is David's heartfelt response to his self-discovery.

Before we look at this in more detail, we need to say something about the book of psalms. This is the Bible's song book, where the people of God have gone since time immemorial, to find songs of praise or experience. Athanasius, the great leader of the church in the fourth century said: 'Most of the Bible speaks *to* us, but the psalms speak *for* us.' They are a vehicle by which God's people are able to express their feelings as they pour out their emotions to God.

We should bear that in mind as we study Psalm 51. It is poetry, reflecting someone's feelings; there is raw emotion here as well as careful thought. David is writing it on his own behalf, but because it's in the Bible it can be used by anyone who is struggling with guilt. Why are we studying Psalm 51? Because up to now we have been looking at the effects of sin upon humanity at large (the Fall); the wrath of God expressed first in exclusion from Paradise and the sentence of death; then the universal judgement (the Flood); we have seen judgement at work upon nations (at the Passover) and we have looked at the atonement ritual for the people of Israel. Today, some scholars want us to believe that sin and salvation in Scripture are to be understood only in corporate ways. Some go so far as to say that the Bible is not about individual guilt, condemnation and forgiveness. But this

Psalm, reflective of David's experience, gives the lie to that. Here we have one man, a member of the covenant community, and the greatest need in his life at this moment is to be forgiven.

The nature of sin

Sin is David's underlying agenda, and he tells us it is *comprehensive* (vs1–3). Once again we find the three words the Bible uses regularly to describe sin:

Sin is a failure to hit the mark, missing the target or a shortcoming of some sort. It conveys the basic idea of a mistake or a failure of thought, word or deed. It is an outward act of wrongdoing. When we look at our lives and think, 'I shouldn't have done that,' that is sin.

Iniquity goes deeper. It goes to the character behind the fault. It has to do with a distortion, a twisting out of shape, a misdirecting or a perverting. It goes to the inward root of corruption from which the outward act of sin flows. The bad things I do are an indicator of the bad that is inside me. I am not bad all the time, no one is, but we do enough bad things to show that there is something out of joint deep inside. Jesus later expounded the meaning of iniquity when he said, 'For out of the heart come evil thoughts, murder, adultery, sexual immorality, theft, false witness, slander' (Mt.15:19 ESV).

Transgressions completes the description. It means wilful rebellion and has to do with a subject rebelling against his rightful lord. Sin is a personal affront offered to God.

Sin is pervasive. David takes our human story back to the point when he was emerging from his mother's womb (v5). Then he takes us back further, to the point in the passion of his parents' lovemaking on the night he was conceived. It was not his parents' act that was sinful but, from the moment of conception, the embryo carried the infection of sin in it. David is saying that, as far back as it is possible to go, he has been in iniquity and sin. Sin is not only a fact of life and experience, it is also a fact of inheritance and personality. It is part of the price of being human.

Some people do not like the language of 'original sin,' preferring instead to talk about humanity's 'original goodness.' But we cannot escape the revelation, given through God's servant David, that we are born with a sinful nature and that each individual is responsible for their own sin. We sin and are conscious that we shouldn't. We have lost our original righteousness. The image of God in humanity has been defaced. And, although we are not all as bad as we could be, we are all, nonetheless, touched by sin in every part of our human nature.

David's sin had been against himself first of all: he had abused his own body by committing adultery with Bathsheba. Paul says that those who commit adultery are sinning against their own bodies. David had also sinned against Bathsheba by using her as a thing, instead of a person, for his own pleasure. And he had sinned against Uriah and engineered his death. But despite all that, sin is primarily *against God*. We have not simply broken a law, we have offended a person: and not just any person. So David quickly confesses 'Against you, you only, have I sinned'. If we do something we know God hates, then we do it to offend him! Sin violates God's standards, so only God can forgive sin. This is why there was uproar among the theologians of Jesus' day when he said to the paralysed man: 'Son, your sins are forgiven.' They saw his underlying claim to be God and thought to themselves: 'He's blaspheming! Who can forgive sins but God alone?' (Mk. 2:1–12).

David goes on to say in verse 4: 'Against you, you only, I have sinned, and done what is evil in your sight, so that you are proved right when you speak and justified when you judge.' The NIV says 'proved right' but it should really say 'so that you are justified'. It's the same word repeated twice; just and justified. Because our sin is against God, there is a penal aspect to it. God is completely 'just' in declaring us humans guilty, and 'justified' in sentencing us to death. David knew he deserved the usual punishment for adultery and murder, which was death. He had 'blood-guilt' on his hands. We have been emphasising this throughout this book, that this is the universal teaching of the Bible, there is this penal aspect to it. Is God unfair when he says that we are sinners, guilty? Is God unfair when he punishes us? David says that his confession of sin actually contributes to the glory of God; it provides the dark background against which we see that God is just. Here is the justification of God; God is just because he calls a spade a spade. He says what is wrong and he punishes sin.

The grace of God

David doesn't just talk about sin, he talks about God – and does so right from the beginning of the psalm (vs1–3). He points to what God is like and talks about God's mercy: 'Have mercy on me.' Mercy has to do with God's favour, with God doing something freely; he is not obliged to do it, and he does it out of his own will. We use the same word in English when we talk about doing each other a favour. And this word falls into the grace vocabulary in the New Testament. It's the same root as the word used when it tells us that God showed grace to Noah in Genesis 6:8. Here is God's free favour shown to people who deserve nothing but his anger.

David also appeals to God's 'unfailing love,' which is connected to his covenant. God's covenant with his people was a covenant in which he said, 'I will love you forever, till death do us part.' This unfailing love of God is a commitment, rooted in the will of the Lover. David is coming before God, conscious of this terrible sin, and trusting in what God has said and what God has committed himself to. He's saying, 'I belong to your people, O God. I have come to trust and believe in you and to become a part of those covenant people that you are in an arrangement with. I'm not arguing about anything in me, because I know what a sinner I am, but I am appealing to something in you, to your covenant love for your people.'

Thirdly, he points to God's compassion (v1). David is appealing to the surging passionate love of God's heart. The word here is also translated 'womb' in the Bible. It is mother love; the compassion a mother feels for her child. It is the compassion a lover feels for her beloved. By appealing to the compassion of God, David is telling us something beautiful about God. He was a man who knew God.

Forgiveness

Why is David talking to God at all in this psalm? Because he knows that only God can forgive sin. The only person whose forgiveness counts is the one who has been hurt, abused, misused; therefore it is from God that he needs forgiveness. All sin is ultimately an offence against God. It is desperately serious.

David uses three different words to describe how God can deal with his sin, and the first one is used in verse 1, where he says that God can 'blot out my transgression'.

Sin leaves a mark that God can see and wipe away. A speeding violation in the UK can result in points being noted on your driving licence. But after three years that record is expunged, it is no longer held against you. That is the sort of language David is using: 'blot out my transgressions' – 'Lord please remove this so that it can't be found again.'

Then he says 'wash away all my iniquity' (v2). Sin permeates to the deepest part of our lives, like dirt getting into the fabric of some cloth. This word is a launderer's word; it means that God reaches the parts that all the other detergents don't reach. God is able to deal with the dirt in our lives. My grandmother had a scrubbing board, a piece of wood with a corrugated side to it. In a deep sink, she would take the clothes and scrub them on the scrubbing board until the ingrained dirt was out of the clothing. David is asking God to scrub him thoroughly, to get the ingrained sin out of his life.

The third word he uses is 'cleanse me' (v2). This word was used of ceremonial purity, and it was built into the mind of the Jewish people through the ceremonial system of priests and tabernacles, as we have seen in earlier chapters. Sin is a barrier between men and women and God; cleansing is the way across the barrier.

When David goes on to say 'You do not take delight in sacrifice' (v16) he is not expressing his dislike of the sacrificial system. In fact, it is quite the reverse. In the Old Testament sin could only be dealt with on the basis of shed blood. David was guilty of adultery and murder, and you can search the Old Testament from beginning to end and you will find that there is no sacrifice ever prescribed which could cleanse someone from the sins of adultery and murder. These were two killer sins; and if someone were found guilty of these sins, they were to be put to death. So David looks at his position in despair:

'You do not take delight in sacrifice.' Where does this leave him? How can the mercy, love and compassion of God help out a man in such a terrible state as this? Can a true believer such as David is, even if he is a sinner, be completely abandoned by the God who has promised to be loyal to his people?

The answer is in verse 7: 'Cleanse me with hyssop and I shall be clean; wash me, and I will be whiter than snow.' When was hyssop first used in the Bible and what was it used for? It was first used at the time of the Passover (Ex. 12). The lamb must be slain, the blood must be gathered, the hyssop must be dipped in the blood, and the blood must be splashed around the door; and then you must go inside and find shelter from the judgement. Hyssop points to a blood sacrifice; it points to a life laid down in payment for sin's penalty, which is death. Hyssop points to a substitute for a sinner. In Egypt, as we have seen, on the night of the Exodus there was a death in every house, without exception. In the houses of the Egyptians the firstborn son died as God judged and punished the sinner. In the houses of the Israelites it was an innocent lamb that died. The blood smeared by the hyssop round the door was an outward and visible sign that in this house a substitute death had taken place and those who went under the shelter of the shed blood were safe.

David wants to be safe from the wrath he knows he deserves. So he says to God, 'Lord, I don't know of any sacrifice that can deal with "blood guilt" (v14) but you know! I ask you to take the hyssop and dip it in the blood you know of, and apply that blood to me. Purge me with hyssop and I shall be clean, wash me and I shall be whiter than snow.' David did not know the blood, but God did.

For if the sprinkling of defiled persons with the blood of goats and bulls and with the ashes of a heifer sanctifies for the purification of the flesh, how much more will the blood of Christ, who through the eternal Spirit offered himself without blemish to God, purify our conscience from dead works to serve the living God (Heb. 9:13–14 ESV).

God knew what would cover David's sin. That's why God said to him through Nathan the prophet, 'You will not die.' David is saying, 'I don't know how you did that. I don't know what this sacrifice that covers blood guilt is.' The New Testament answers David's cry. The blood of Jesus Christ, God's son, cleanses us from all sin. This is the mercy of God. This is the product of the loving kindness of God for his people, this is the outgrowth of his tender compassion. God did not spare his own Son but delivered him up freely on his own behalf. There is deep cleansing that reaches parts that all of the other sacrifices could never reach. It removes the sin that bars us from God's presence; it wipes the slate clean so that I do not stand condemned before him. This is what the hyssop does. It cleans me through the blood of Christ and it brings joy and gladness (v8) back where the bones have been crushed.

Repentance

Repentance is a matter of spiritual renewal. In verses 10–12, the second half of each verse mentions the spirit. What we need is a renewed or 'right' spirit (v10 ESV), the 'Holy Spirit' (v11), and a 'willing spirit' (v12). The expression in verse 10 is variously translated 'upright' or 'right', but literally it means 'perpendicular.' We have gone off the perpendicular and are 'way off beam.' Once we sin, we get into the habit of sinning and we need help. This will require a new creation: 'Create in me a clean heart, O God' (v10 ESV). In other words, true repentance never comes naturally. It will take the work of God in us to make us see where we have done wrong.

This is the real problem with us. We don't see the exceeding sinfulness of sin. It is a light thing to us, very often, to have broken God's laws. We minimise the seriousness of our bad behaviour and even persuade ourselves that our particular sins are small and insignificant compared to other people. And sometimes they are, especially when we compare ourselves to a mass murderer! But that is not the issue. It is against God we have sinned, it is he whom we have offended, and that is a big issue of eternal implications.

Repentance is also a matter of personal confession. David is entirely honest in his admittance of his wrongdoing: 'For I know my transgressions and my sin is always before me' (v3). Note the emphatic personal pronouns; 'I acknowledge *my* rebellion.' Repentance is a matter of personal confession. He admits to being a sinner generally and he gets down to admitting his specific sin of 'blood-guiltiness' in verse 14 (ESV). David actually *felt* that he had grieved God and now it was grieving him that he had done so. How dare he ask for forgiveness for these terrible crimes? He dares to ask because he acknowledges his sin. Our confession is the link between the cleansing which God can give on the basis of Christ's death, and the heart of the sinner which needs to be cleansed.

David is now ready to make a radical decision – and to stop sinning. This is the way to true joy. It's like someone saying to you after you've hurt them, 'That's all right' and knowing they mean it. No wonder 'joy and gladness' are restored. What Nathan actually said to David was, 'The LORD has removed your sin. You will not die.'

This Psalm takes us a step further in the Bible's unfolding drama of redemption. It shows us that individuals need to have their own sin cancelled by God; that they need to have the blood of the sacrifice applied to their own guilty conscience; that they must have a sacrifice which will prevent them from suffering the ultimate penalty for sin – eternal death. But which sacrifice? What animal or number of animals could ever atone for the sins of blood-guilt or any other sins for that matter? How could God possibly remove David's sin?

Act 2 Scene 2

Wounded for me

What has happened in our story so far? We have seen the entrance of sin into the world and its devastating consequences. Death is the indicator that everyone is under the penalty of sin. We have seen that sin provokes the wrath of God, first in the judgement of the world by a flood, and then in the plagues that swept through Egypt. What can be done? From the earliest point and with increasing clarity, we have discovered that the only hope is in the blood sacrifice of an innocent victim, as in the lambs at Passover, the sacrifices of the Day of Atonement and the whole ritual of Judaism. But these sacrifices cannot deal with all sin, as we saw in David's case. Something more effective is required and David looks forward to it. What could possibly be a sacrifice equivalent to the life of any human being?

Isaiah 53 takes us one step nearer the final truth; only someone sent by God who is pure and has no sins of his own to answer for can take our place and bear our punishment. Back in Genesis there was a hint of a human sacrifice when Abraham took Isaac out to the mountain to kill him in obedience to God's word. This shocks us when we read it: what was God thinking? But the clue is in the finale: 'The Lord will provide a lamb, my son,' says Abraham. We are still waiting, and here in Isaiah the lamb is introduced to us.

The upside-down kingdom

The 2006 Boston University in London annual lecture was given by Professor Peter Hawkins, the Professor of Religion and Literature there. It was on the Bible as literature and its effect on the English language. He commented that many of those who come to study the Bible at Boston assume they know what it means. He cited evangelicals, in particular, who are sure they know what the Bible means – even though they have never read it. Then he went on to describe the different gospels that are gaining currency: for instance, the prosperity gospel, the self-esteem gospel and the therapeutic gospel.

Commenting on the prosperity gospel, he said the idea that following Jesus leads to success and triumph cannot be sustained from Jesus' own teaching. Anyone who has ever listened to the teaching of Jesus Christ will be struck by his emphasis on suffering as the way to glory, and death as the way to life. Jesus' priorities run counter to the ways of the world that wants its heroes to be tough not weak: to win, not to lose. If success is the criterion for heroism, then Jesus doesn't qualify to be a hero in the world's eyes.

Listen to some of the things Jesus said: 'The Son of Man did not come to be served but to serve and to give his life as a ransom for many.' Or 'The Son of Man must suffer many things and be rejected by the elders and the chief priests and the teachers of the law and he must be killed and on the third day raised to life.' Or 'Then he opened up their minds so that they could understand the Scriptures and told them, "This is what is written: The Christ the Messiah will suffer and rise from the dead on the third day."' These examples of Jesus' sayings tell us three things: firstly, that he understood his destiny to be suffering and death. Secondly, that he learned his destiny from the Bible and thirdly, that he had resolved to fulfil that destiny voluntarily, without coercion.

But which Scriptures guided his view of his role and destiny? Some we have seen already in this book: Genesis 3, the Passover lamb in Exodus, and the Day of Atonement in Leviticus. But none is so clear and so profound in its implication as this passage in Isaiah 53.

The great German Professor Joachim Jeremais put it like this: 'No other passage from the Old Testament was as important to the church as Isaiah 53.'[18] And it was important to the church because it was important to Jesus. Eight out of its twelve verses are quoted in the New Testament. Jesus quotes from verse 12 in Luke 22 when he says: 'For I tell you that this Scripture must be fulfilled in me: "And He was numbered among the transgressors"' (ESV) and he comments that what is written about him had been fulfilled. When he says that he had come not to be served but to serve and to be a ransom for many, he is echoing this chapter. In Acts 8:34 when Philip finds an Ethiopian official reading from the Old Testament Scriptures, he is reading out of Isaiah; 'Then Philip began with that very passage of Scripture and told him the good news about Jesus.' John Stott wrote: 'Every verse in the chapter except verse 2 is applied to Jesus in the New Testament, some verses several times. Indeed there is good evidence that Jesus' whole public career, from his baptism through his ministry, sufferings and death to his resurrection and ascension, is seen as the fulfilment of the pattern foretold in Isaiah 53.'[19]

Already in Isaiah the description of God's Servant has carried with it the overture of suffering (50:6). But here it is taken further; the suffering is explained as the wounding and bruising of one who bore the sins of others. After this, Zion is called into a covenant of peace (54:10) and the whole world into an everlasting covenant (55:3).

Isaiah is addressing the nation nearly seven hundred years before Jesus appears. The nation is a privileged and holy nation, that God has called, and yet in spite of all its privileges, it has turned its back on them and gone off into blatant immorality. The nation has disqualified itself from being described as God's holy people. Sin is the problem and Isaiah is addressing those who will come under the approaching judgement. As he looks into this troubled future, Isaiah tells them about the coming of the figure whom he calls 'the Servant' and this passage marks the high point in his description of him.

The exalted one is humbled

Who is this Servant about whom Isaiah speaks? In 52:13–15, it's as if he's saying, 'I want the spotlight now on my Servant.' Someone has come on the stage to do a little soliloquy. There is a voice-over to prepare us for what's coming next: 'Get ready. Have your eyes peeled. My Servant, that's the person to look out for.' Verse 13: 'My servant will act wisely', that is, he will accomplish his purpose. He will both know and do the right thing in order to accomplish that to which he is called. People may think he has failed, but he will not and God wants that to be known.

The Servant will not only be humbled, he will also be exalted (v13). This parallels the story of Jesus, who is raised in his resurrection, lifted up through his ascension to heaven, and highly exalted when he sits down at the right hand of the Majesty in Heaven.

Isaiah has already used this phraseology four times, and everywhere else it describes God himself. The most famous place is in Isaiah 6, where Isaiah goes into the Temple and says, 'I saw the Lord seated on a throne, high and exalted, and the train of his robe filled the temple. Above him were seraphs . . . And they were calling to one another: "Holy, holy, holy is the LORD Almighty; the whole earth is full of his glory."' Wherever this phrase is used, it is used exclusively of God; so what is used of God is also used of Jesus. In fact, in the New Testament, Isaiah 6 is quoted with this comment, 'Isaiah said these things because he saw his (Jesus') glory and spoke of him' (Jn.12:41). This language of exaltation is taken out of Isaiah and applied directly to the Lord Jesus by the apostle Paul. Philippians 2, Paul's famous hymn about Christ that was sung by the early Christians, echoes the two themes that are here. Paul talks about the Christ; the Messiah taking the form of a Servant and being humbled, and that God has highly exalted him and given him 'the name that is above every name' (v9).

Isaiah reverses that process, beginning by telling us that this Servant will be exalted, but also that in his humiliation he will be brought very low. Verse 14 of Isaiah 52 says 'many . . . were appalled at him – his appearance was so disfigured beyond that of any man and his form marred beyond human likeness.' Modern-day heroes are good-looking; but this Servant was not impressive. There is shock and horror at his appearance. Many were astonished; this 'many' in verse 14 stands in sharp contrast to the one, the Servant. The many are appalled; the one is disfigured. That word 'appalled' means, 'shocked, shattered, devastated' by what they see.

They are repelled by what they see; appalled at his scarred face and torn body; they look at him and think he is hardly even human. In fact, the important people, the kings of this world (v15) are amazed at his humiliation. No one had ever thought that the rescuer and deliverer would be someone who was so terribly lowly. Paul picks up this language in 1 Corinthians 2 when he talks about the greatest and the wisest of the world who did not expect this Servant to act in this way. He says, 'None of the rulers of this age understood it, or if they had they would never have crucified the Lord of Glory.'

Yet, in spite of this, he still makes an impact. 'He will sprinkle many nations.' The word 'sprinkled' here is a Hebrew word used many times in the Hebrew Bible, but some scholars prefer an Arabic word, 'startle', which is similar in form. The only problem is that that is never used in the Old Testament and so is a less likely interpretation. But, either way, it doesn't change the impact of the words. The overall idea is that just as many are appalled at him, many are going to benefit from him, and the likelihood is that the word is sprinkle and refers to the Servant's work being a priestly work, a sign of the sacrifice being made.

The Promised One is rejected

The Servant, or promised one, is first described as 'the arm of the Lord.' The Bible often uses physical descriptions of God. God doesn't have arms, he is Spirit, but the Bible uses anthromorphisms (using human terms to explain God). God doesn't have arms but he has a 'mighty arm' to accomplish his will: he can do for us what we cannot do for ourselves. Isaiah has talked about the arm of God. In the Exodus, it was God himself who *with his mighty arm* brought the children of Israel out of their bondage into liberty (Is. 51:9–10). In Isaiah 52:10 the arm is bared again as he gets ready to do something truly dramatic and powerful. The arm of the Lord has been revealed. We might expect to find it to be an 'arm' of military might, political influence or numerical superiority. But its revelation will surprise us.

Whenever this expression is used in Scripture it always has overtones of power and triumph. Surely that is what we must expect here? Instead, Isaiah focuses on the weakness of the Servant (Is. 53:2–3). When this arm appears, it appears like a tender shoot and a root out of dry ground. You're expecting power, and you see a tiny little shoot, vulnerable, unobtrusive. What's Isaiah saying? When the arm of the Lord is revealed, when the promised Servant comes, people will not naturally look at him and say, 'That's the leader.' At Christmas when he came into the world as a baby, sucking at his mother's breast and lying in a manger, there was no pomp and circumstance to mark the occasion. Nothing! Look at verse 2: 'He had no beauty or majesty to attract us to him, nothing in his appearance that we should desire him.' In fact, people will not believe it. Only by revelation could people ever come to see that this one, who is so humbly born, so unimpressive in appearance, could yet be the arm of God. This is a description of how people come to faith. It starts with revelation: that revelation is proclaimed through a message and people come to believe the message.

When Isaiah says, 'He was despised' (v3) it means to be regarded as of little value, not worth thinking or talking about. Jesus was despised and rejected. People thought that he had no relevance to them whatsoever, especially because he had his own troubles. 'He was despised and rejected by men, a man of sorrows'. Why should we take him seriously when he has troubles enough of his own? When you want someone to rescue you, you don't want someone from the same cell; you want someone from the outside. But Jesus is in the same cell as us. And so 'He was despised, and we esteemed him not.' That word 'esteemed' is an accounting word, meaning that he added up to nothing. The authentic Jesus doesn't measure up to our normal ideas of success, or celebrity or strength, which is why we find it hard to accept him as he is. We don't want to be in the minority. That is why we hate the way of Jesus by nature because we prefer the way of success, power and influence. And just as today people are beguiled by the doctrine of health and wealth, so in the past Christians have been beguiled by the idea of success, influence and power, and even political and territorial superiority. But they weren't acting as Christians; they were simply following the world's philosophy. Here is Jesus, and this arm of God will surprise us. In fact many will not believe it. Hence the question: who has believed the message and to whom has the arm of the Lord been revealed? Not many.

The substituted one punished

At the heart of the passage we discover God in action through the work of the substitute, who is acting alone. He is 'pierced for our transgressions . . . crushed for our iniquities'. The whole emphasis in verses 4–6 is on his suffering. He suffers but not because of anything he has done wrong. In fact, we've got it all wrong when we think he is suffering for his own sin: 'we considered him stricken by God.' There can be no avoiding the fact that the Servant acts as a substitute on behalf of others. Ours are the griefs, sorrows, transgressions, iniquities; he is the one 'stricken, smitten by God, and afflicted.'

Isaiah 53 says explicitly what has been implicit up to now, that sin is an offence against God. He takes it seriously; it provokes his wrath and he will punish it himself. Sin requires spiritual punishment. This is infinitely more serious than earthly or temporal punishment. Alienation from God is so serious that the sacrificial system was introduced to teach us that an innocent sacrifice must die if we are ever to have fellowship with God again. There can be no escaping the point: it is God himself who punishes the Servant as he stands in for his people. Isaiah says later, 'it was the will of the Lord to crush him' (Is. 53:10 ESV).

This is what we call 'penal substitution,' a substitute suffering the penalty due to another. But the question remains, 'Can a sheep die for a man?' 'Can a goat die for a woman?' In the end an animal cannot act as a substitute for a person. But a perfect man could. The lamb of God could. The gospel writer, John, introduces Jesus with these words, 'Behold, the lamb of God who takes away the sin of the world' (Jn. 1:29). This Servant suffers for the people so that they do not ever need to suffer the consequences of their sins. What happens to the Servant? He is 'pierced through' or 'wounded.' This word refers in the strongest terms to an excruciating and violent death. It is also consistent with the wounds inflicted on Jesus on the Cross. 'Crushed' means pulverised. The language emphasises how seriously God takes sin.

We typically wish to make light of our 'shortcomings,' to explain away our 'mistakes.' But God will have none of it. The refusal of humanity to bow to the Creator's rule, and our insistence on drawing up our own moral codes that pander to our lusts, are not shortcomings or mistakes. They are the stuff of death and corruption, and unless someone can be found to stand in our place, they will see us impaled on the swords of our own making, broken on the racks of our own design.[20]

Verses 4–5 are rich in metaphors of disease and rebellion. They precisely echo Isaiah 1:5–6. There the nation is described as in rebellion and therefore full of open sores and exposed wounds. What they need is someone to come and wipe the slate clean; someone to take the disease and bring true spiritual healing; someone to take the punishment and give true peace.

Shalom is absolute 'well-being.' We don't enjoy such peace because everything is out of order. All our good intentions and our best works cannot bring it back. Our relationship with God has been disrupted and his sense of justice offended. What he wants is for the relationship to be restored and justice to be satisfied.

So what has God done about it? 'We all, like sheep, have gone astray, each of us has turned to his way; and the Lord has laid on him the iniquity of us all' (v6). Lying at the very heart of the Christian message is the self-substitution of God. Here is a divine act of concentrating in one place, onto one substituted victim, the sin of all the sinners that God has purposed to save. The substituted one is punished.

The innocent one is slaughtered

The substituted one is also the innocent one. Verse 7 talks about his voluntary acceptance of the role: the silence of willing submission. He is oppressed and afflicted, yet he does not open his mouth in self-defence. Why? Because he is standing in our place, he is going to take our sin on himself; he will not evade what lies ahead because we are on his heart. He sets his face to go to Jerusalem. He is led like a lamb to the slaughter.

And he faces the oppressiveness of judicial procedures (v8). He experiences injustice. The account of Jesus' trials in the gospels proves that it was a complete show trial: every rule of Jewish procedural law was broken. This Servant does not deserve the punishment of his people, he did not deserve any punishment at all. 'He had done no violence, nor was any deceit in his mouth' (v9).

The weak one is glorified

There is always something terribly compelling about the story of the innocent sufferer. It leaves so many questions up in the air and it's the same here. Is this an accident? Was this beyond God's control? What did Jesus' suffering achieve? Isaiah rounds off this poem with the conclusion that the Servant is satisfied at this work. Look at how he puts it: 'It was the Lord's will to crush him and cause him to suffer and though the Lord makes his life a guilt offering, he will see his offspring and prolong his days.'

He's done to death (v9), but in verse 10 he sees his offspring and prolongs his days. In verse 9 he's dead, and in verse 10 he's alive. In verse 9 he's finished, in verse 10 he's looking at the effective results of all that he's accomplished. We looked at the words of Jesus earlier from John 17 when he says to his Father, before he's even gone to the cross, 'I have glorified you on earth by finishing the work that you gave me to do.' Here is the Lord Jesus, and he sees the fruit of his death. The writer of Hebrews talks about Jesus seeing before him the joy of many sons and daughters being in glory with him. Isaiah tells us, 'After the suffering of his soul, he will see the light of life and be satisfied; by his knowledge my righteous servant will justify many, and he will bear their iniquities.'

Not only will he see life, but he'll give us life. He'll be satisfied with the work that he's done. We think of the words on the cross: 'Finished!' 'Accomplished!' 'Done.' The work that he came to do is completed. In verse 12 everything is summed up by this triumphal exultation: 'I will give him a portion among the great.' That word 'great' should probably be translated by the word 'many.' It's the same word as 'many' elsewhere in the passage. The verse continues: 'he shall divide the spoil with the strong, because he poured out his soul to death and was numbered with the transgressors; yet he bore the sin of many, and makes intercession for the transgressors.'

This was the kind of thing that was on Jesus' mind. Before that moment of standing before Pilate in the judgement hall, this is on Jesus' mind. Before they took him and pierced him and put the nails into his wrist, this is on his mind. What is the only proper response to what this suffering Servant achieved? Isaiah immediately goes on to apply this in chapter 54: 'Sing,' he says. It is time for joy because of what this Servant has achieved. 'Shout for joy, you people,' he says. 'Enlarge the place of your tent. Realise that something's going to happen that's going to break all the boundaries.' Then in 55:1 he applies it to everyone and he says, 'Come, all you who are thirsty, come to the waters; and you who have no money, come, buy and eat.' 'Listen! Listen to me! Eat what is good and your soul will delight in the richest of fare. I'll make an everlasting covenant with you.'

Good news. The God we have offended by our sin is the God who loves you and the evidence is the work of the suffering Servant. God's last word is to invite all who are thirsty to come and have their thirst quenched by the Lord Jesus.

Act 2 Scene 3

The main event

The drama is moving to its climax. The main act is about to begin; the story of the Passion of Christ – his crucifixion and resurrection. In each of the gospels we are introduced to the Saviour, shown his credentials and then pointed to his work. The mere arrangement of the material as well as the teaching of the text emphasises that his whole life's work finds its focus at the end, as he moves to the cross.

Pick up the average biography of some great personality – a military person, an actor or politician – and look in the index for the account of their death. Turn to the last few pages of the book and you'll be lucky to find a page or a paragraph. But when you turn to the four gospels, you'll discover that in each of them one-third of the book is occupied by telling the story of Jesus' death. And within a few years of the Christian movement being launched, the symbol that they choose is none other than the executioner's gallows, the cross. Not the nice gold cross around your girlfriend or wife's neck, not the kind of cross we see outside our churches, but that rough wooden cross with which the people of the day were familiar outside their towns and villages. It was an offensive symbol of a terrible way to end the life of the lowest form of humanity, the worst offenders.

Mark is probably the earliest of our four gospels, and he is writing at a fast pace. He's in a hurry to get to the climax, the most important part of his story. He very quickly introduces us to the characters and major events in the life of Jesus, beginning with his public ministry. In particular, he introduces us to Jesus by showing him fulfilling the three main offices of ancient Judaism, that of the prophet, the priest and the king.

He begins with Jesus as a prophet. As you read Mark, Jesus speaks the word of God and people are amazed at the authority with which he speaks. Then Mark introduces us to Jesus as a priest. He goes into the temple of God and finds that it is being turned into a marketplace. Those who are meant to be looking out for the needs of the people are in fact lining their own pockets. He challenges them, overturns the tables, throws out the money changers and cleanses the temple, all as the righteous priest.

And he comes as King. When people come with a coin from Rome with Caesar's head on and ask him the question 'Whose inscription and whose image is this?', Jesus thwarts their attempt to trip him up and challenges them on whether they will give him authority over their souls. Caesar had the right to their tax, but he has the right to their allegiance. He has come as a prophet, a priest and a King, and these three offices come together as we near the end.

Jesus in the limelight

In Mark 15, the main character of the drama takes the stage. We haven't seen him since the first act, John 17, we've only heard the rumours of him but now he is in the spotlight – and the story seems on the surface to be going wrong.

The prophet is silenced

Jesus, the prophet, is arrested and taken before the Sanhedrin, the Jewish ruling council. After interrogating him, the high priest is infuriated by him. He tears his clothes and says, 'Why do we need any more witnesses? This man has committed blasphemy,' and he condemns him as deserving death. Some spit on him, they blindfold him, strike him with their fists and say 'Prophesy' and the guards beat him. 'Prophesy. Go on, Messiah,' they say, 'Tell us who hit you.' They are deliberately rejecting Jesus in his role as prophet, the one who brings the word of God to them.

The king is mocked

When Jesus is handed over to the secular authorities, his claim to be the Messiah is equally rejected, but this time the focus of the rejection is his claim to be king.

Firstly, Jesus is given a Roman whipping. What we know about this scourging has been well represented in Mel Gibson's *The Passion*. In fact, if anything, Mel Gibson held back on the details. It would have been even more horrific than the film's depiction. Frequently, victims would die as a result of the whipping they received and Jesus is weakened by it. Having been cruelly flogged, Jesus is now led away to be held by the Roman soldiers.

These men display one of the most frightening traits in the human personality: discipline of unusual degree in one area and gross moral indiscipline in another. There is something particularly grotesque about their little game. They have called their fellow soldiers together for an hour of entertainment with Jesus. Utterly alone, humiliated and virtually naked, Jesus is set in front of them in mock-regal dress – a crown of thorns and a purple robe. They call him 'King of the Jews' while spitting on him and striking him on the head. 'They mocked him', says Mark (v20) until the time comes to lead him to the place where he would be crucified. They would show Jesus what they really thought of his claims. They do not have the eyes to see that the only thing they are doing is fulfilling to the letter the manifesto Jesus has earlier published among his disciples (Mk. 9:31). Even in the hour of his deepest humiliation, he is reigning as king.

At this stage in the proceedings leading finally to the crucifixion, a man might be too weakened to carry the beam of the cross on which he would be impaled. The soldiers therefore press-gang a man named Simon, from Cyrene, to carry the beam. Mark mentions his sons, Alexander and Rufus, which seems to indicate that they were known to the first readers of the gospel – and if so had presumably become Christians. The story of their conversion was perhaps so well known that Mark did not need to say any more. If so, he could have given no clearer hint of the power of God's kingdom than this – in his weakest hour, Jesus began his reign of grace in one home and family.

The king must remain in control of his faculties, and so Jesus refuses the wine mixed with myrrh, given as a drink to relieve the terrible pain of crucifixion. Even now the messianic prophecies continue to be fulfilled: as the crowd watch, the soldiers cast lots for his clothing (Ps. 22:18).

Earlier in the gospel, Mark records the request of James and John to be at Jesus' right hand and his left. They did not understand the cup he would drink and the baptism he would experience. Now two others are at his right hand and his left; these men, along with those who pass by and the religious leaders, pour similar contempt on him. They despise him as prophet ('You who are going to destroy the temple and build it in three days' v29); they mock him as priest ('He saved others . . . he cannot save himself'); they humiliate him as king ('Let this Christ, this King of Israel, come down now from the cross, that we may see and believe' v32). How blind they are to what is actually happening. Only if Jesus refuses to save himself could he save others. The very words they speak could have brought them to the heart of the gospel. But they could not understand God's ways or recognise his Messiah, even when above him were the words: 'The king of the Jews' (v26).

Jesus must have often considered this moment. As early as Mark 2:20, he had spoken of how he would be 'taken' from his disciples. As he had come nearer to that event, he had explained its significance to them: he would be rejected, would suffer and die in a cruel and humiliating fashion. None of this was unexpected; all of it was under his control. Crucified as king, he was king still. He made the cross his first throne.

'You who were going to destroy the temple and build it in three days.' If only they had taken into account what they were saying, they would find themselves exposed to the very heart of the Christian message, that he *was* King of the Jews, that he *was* speaking the word of God, he was going to fulfil his prediction. They were going to destroy the temple and Jesus would be raised in three days. Jesus himself was the temple, the place in which God lived and dwelled. And instead of not saving himself, he was going to save them by not saving himself. That was going to become obvious in the days that followed.

As the messianic prophet, Jesus has been despised and abused; as the messianic king, he has been mocked and enthroned on a Roman gibbet. Now Mark shows us that as the messianic priest he becomes the sacrificial victim for the sins of his people.

The unnatural darkness

Jesus' crucifixion takes place during the Jewish festival of Passover. As he hangs on the cross, a strange darkness comes over the land. Mark does not explain its significance to us. Perhaps he assumes that his readers have followed the course of events and will make a connection between this darkness and the celebration of Passover.

In the Exodus from Egypt, the plague of darkness had been God's last word to Pharaoh before the judgement of God visited the land. The sign of darkness was a sign that God was withdrawing his grace and favour from the world. To be cast into darkness means to be exposed to the anger of God. Does that surprise us? When we talk about anger, we often mean something wild, unpredictable and usually undeserved. However, in the Bible, God's anger is measured and most definitely deserved. The very existence of death in the world is evidence that every one of us is under the condemnation of God because of our sinful rebellion against him. To us, sin is a light thing. We get upset by big bad things like the 9/11 or 7/7 atrocities. But, to God, jealousy, adultery, selfishness and godlessness are sin also and all sin leaves us cut off from him. The plague of darkness was a wake-up call for everyone to get ready because God was on the move, and unless they repented, God was going to judge. And the next thing that happened was the death of the firstborn in every house in Egypt.

Now it is the turn of God's firstborn to die! As Jesus hangs on the cross, that darkness is a wake-up call to those who are looking on. The darkness is the thing that preceded the judgement, only this time it isn't going to be any other son that's going to die, this time it's going to be God's own Son that will die. Here is God giving himself in his Son to take the judgement that is coming on the world, and to absorb that judgement in himself on the cross. This darkness, which has an Old Testament background, is a symbol of the wrath of God. God is angry at sin. He is not angry at Jesus, but he is angry at sin and here Jesus is bearing our sin.

In Exodus a Passover lamb was taken and killed. Instead of the firstborn son dying – whether they were Jews and Egyptians or whatever they were – they took refuge in a place that was covered by the blood of that Passover lamb and their firstborn was spared death. Death itself is the sign that we're under the wrath of God. The soul that sins, it shall die. The wages of sin is death.

The spiritual agony

This is why the terrible cry of dereliction issued from Christ's lips: 'Eloi, Eloi, lama sabachthani?' which means 'My God, my God, why have you forsaken me?' This was something he had never ever known. From all eternity he had enjoyed a perfect relationship of perfect love with his Father. Back in John 17 we heard Jesus say, 'Father, I desire that they also, whom you have given me, may be with me where I am, to see my glory that you have given me . . . that the love with which you have loved me may be in them, and I in them' (ESV). Throughout his life on earth he had only ever lived to please him and serve him. And his Father had returned the compliment; Jesus is standing in the waters of baptism by the River Jordan and the Father says from heaven. 'This is my beloved Son; with him I am well pleased.' All through his life, whenever Jesus refers to God, he calls God, 'Father' – except now. Here his Father has abandoned him.

When Jesus cries out, 'My God . . . why have you forsaken me?' he is experiencing what is involved in being the sin-bearer in the presence of the sinless God. As he comes before God as the high priest of his people, he carries no other substitutionary sacrifice for them, he brings only himself. He is both the priest and the victim. There is a connection here with the Day of Atonement. On the Day of Atonement, as we have seen, the high priest would take two animals: one he would kill and the other he would lay his hands on, as a symbolic gesture that all of the sins of people were laid on this animal. Someone would take the animal out into the desert and abandon it there. Here is Jesus fulfilling that picture and experiencing that abandonment. He is taking our sin away, out of sight. God is removing it. He is saying that 'For those who trust in my Son, I will never ever again hold their sin against them.' Here is Jesus being abandoned by God for the sake of his people.

In many ways this is an insight into hell. What is hell ultimately but being abandoned by God? Not that he does this arbitrarily. He intervenes in our lives and speaks through our circumstances. He exposes us to his truth. And we resist it. We are not persuaded that he exists; not sure that if he exists he is worth bothering about; not at all impressed that he loves us. So there comes the day of judgement, when God will say to us, 'You have shown that you would rather live without me, without my influence or my love. I will let you have what you want for all eternity.' That is hell; to be shut up to the choice we have made against God for all eternity.

Why then is Jesus abandoned? It isn't because of his sin: he has none. It is because of our sin. He is dying in our place, bearing our penalty. Jesus is paying the price of sin so that we might never have to.

Many of those who watched these events misunderstood his cry. They thought he must be calling for Elijah, because his words in Hebrew were 'Eloi, Eloi' (v34). Apparently many people thought in those days that Elijah was the patron saint of sufferers. That is why someone decided to offer him a drink, perhaps to perk him up a bit, keep the entertainment going, and see what else he might say. As they stood there watching, they were taking part in the most important event in human history, and yet they seem blind to what is really going on. Their minds were clouded with superstition. If they had known the Scripture as well as they knew popular religion, they would have remembered Psalm 22 which Jesus was quoting. There they would have learned the true meaning of his death.

The torn curtain

Another event takes us even closer to the truth of what is going on here. The curtain of the temple is torn from top to bottom. The temple is where the Jewish people met with God; it was the official residence of God we might say, the place where God would meet with his people. And in this temple was a curtain. This was not like a pair of curtains you might buy from a department store. This was a huge thing, thirty feet high, made from one bit of material and as thick as a man's hand. It was woven into one piece of work and was substantial. It was there in the temple as a perpetual reminder to the people that there was a barrier between them and God. It was a 'No Entry' sign. That curtain kept everyone out of the place where God was present. Here is Jesus on the cross, and the curtain is torn from the top to the bottom. God, in this dramatic action, is saying that the barrier has been removed by what Jesus has done on the cross. The 'Keep Out' sign has been taken down. The temple now stood desecrated by God himself. Jesus had opened a new way into God's presence.

The torn curtain proclaims to us that there is now a sure way to God. It tells us that we can be totally accepted by him through believing what Jesus has done. Why is his work so sure? It is because once the judgement has fallen on him, it cannot fall again on us. Anyone who comes to God via Jesus Christ can come right into the very place where God is pleased to meet with his people, into the very throne room of God, and can have a relationship with him. How is that possible? Because once the judgement has fallen, you cannot be judged again. And because the judgement fell on Jesus, it cannot fall on us.

Quite a few years ago our younger son Andrew and I went to investigate a fire that someone had started in a park near where we live. We were feeling very responsible and decided that we should try and put the fire out, but it kept on moving towards us and the smoke was getting into our eyes. I lifted Andrew over the flames into the burnt area and jumped over beside him. Once we were on the burnt ground on the other side of the flames, we were able to put the fire out without any trouble at all.

We were safe there because once the fire has burned the ground, it cannot burn it again.

Because Jesus has already endured the judgement of God, anyone who puts their trust in Jesus is standing on the burnt ground of Calvary. The judgement has passed; there is no fear of judgement any more. That's why Christians can say 'No condemnation now I dread', because the work has been done by Jesus on the cross. Those who trust in Christ can never come into condemnation again.

The numerous witnesses

These events on Calvary are central to the story of Jesus and were witnessed by bystanders. The Roman centurion's response is important. As he stood by, he heard something that was probably unique in his experience: a crucified man crying out with a loud voice, and dying (v37). Why was that so significant? Because crucified men often took two days or longer to die. It was a death of prolonged agony and increasing weakness. Crucified men simply did not cry out with loud voices. They had no strength to do so. 'And when the centurion, who stood there in front of Jesus, heard this cry and saw how he died, he said, "Surely this man was the Son of God!"' (Mk. 15:39).

We don't know what the soldier meant by the words he used but Mark records them and invites us to make them our own. Over and over again in his gospel, he gets us to come back to this question: Who is Jesus? Here, in his weakness and rejection, Jesus is seen to be none other than the Son of God. Mark records it here because he wants us to consider how Jesus died. He wants us to think about why this is the heart of the Christian

message. Why don't we major on his kindness to
the weak and his love for the poor? Notice that all
those things are absolutely true of him, and we celebrate
them, but this is what the gospel writers went on
about: his death. Because his death changes the world for
us!

Mark also tells us that Jesus' death was witnessed,
from a distance, by a group of women who had
ministered to him and the disciples in Galilee (vs40–41),
as well as by others. These women reappear in Mark's
narrative at Jesus' burial and then as witnesses of the
empty tomb. They saw him die; they saw the tomb where
he was laid (v47); and they saw the stone rolled away on
the first Easter morning.

Why does Mark refer to them here? Because they were
witnesses to the central facts of the Christian Gospel
which were enshrined in the great creeds and hymns of
the Christian church, as well as in the rest of the New
Testament. You can be sure of them because there were
people there to verify the events. Jesus 'suffered under
Pontius Pilate, was crucified, died and was buried . . . on
the third day he rose from the dead' (The Apostles
Creed). The true priest had entered into the presence of
God on our behalf, bearing the sacrifice for our sins –
himself. Soon he would emerge, in full view of his
people, his work completed, his sacrifice accepted, and
communion with God restored.

Why such an emphasis on the death of Jesus? We are
told why in Mark 10:45: 'For even the Son of Man did not
come to be served, but to serve, and to give his life as a
ransom for many.' The word used here for ransom means
a rescue or release secured by payment of a price. It
'always meant a substitutionary-offering for a human
life.'[21] The preposition 'for' (Greek: anti) means 'in place
of' or 'instead of' or 'in exchange for.'

The Son of Man came, by his own decision, into the world to do the job. There is a sense of mission that echoes the kind of language we have already seen in Isaiah 53. He came to give himself as a ransom. The ransom price is paid and that ransom price is equivalent to those people who he rescued.

When Jesus is on the cross, he's acting as our substitute. Jesus dies instead of us; Jesus takes the punishment instead of me having to be punished. Jesus bears my penalty, my sin and my guilt. There's nothing left but for me to go free because I've been ransomed by the blood of Jesus.

Here is the good news for us. Sin is like slavery, captivity. We cannot break out of it on our own. We need someone to break in from the outside and rescue us. To get us out a price is required. Someone must take the punishment due to us; someone must die in my place. Christ is that someone. As a result of what he has done, we get to go free.

Act 3 Scene 1

The Cross examined

If everything in eternity and history moved forward towards the cross, then everything now flows out from it towards history's ultimate climax. In Act 3, we will see how the early Christians understood that main event for a world that had never seen its like and, ultimately, we will be given an insight into the grand finale of the story which is also the end of *our* story.

Scene 1 begins somewhere near the Forum in ancient Rome. A messenger carries a precious document; a letter from one of the leading figures in a new movement which has burst on to the stage somewhere in the middle of the first century. It was first read to a mixed group of people from around the Mediterranean basin, who had come to Rome to make their fortune but had found instead the Saviour of the world. By the time they get this letter, the fledgling Christian movement has broken out of its Palestinian homeland and has touched the centre of the world, mighty Rome itself. The people who heard it read for the first time found themselves often misunderstood for their commitment to a Jewish Messiah and

106

abused for their faith in a crucified Saviour. Romans could think of nothing more sinister or revolting than crucifixion, nor more threatening than a movement which made a cross the centre of its message. The apostle Paul writes to them to explain and defend the gospel itself. The message of these 'apostles' was important because, as Jesus taught in John 17, the rest of the Christian story would be that of people who come to believe in him through their message.

Romans has been called the greatest of all the New Testament letters and it certainly is the clearest statement of the gospel ever. Luther and Calvin saw it as the gateway to the Bible. And if Romans is the greatest statement of the gospel, then verses 3:21–31 are pivotal. Martin Luther called them 'the chief point, and the very central place of the Epistle, and of the whole Bible.'[22] Leon Morris says they may be 'possibly the most important single paragraph ever written.'[23] Their importance is caught in the first words: 'But now'!

The Christian message must have appeared a very small thing to believe in, in comparison to mighty Rome and her armies. So Paul writes why he is 'not ashamed of the gospel (1:16), saying 'Whatever pressures are on you, don't give it up. You have heard of my sufferings, what has kept me from coming to see you, how I've been attacked, stripped and beaten, and all of these things that have happened on account of my commitment to the gospel. But in spite of everything that's occurred to me, everything that has gone wrong since I became a preacher, all the opposition that I've faced from within and without the church, I want you to know I'm not ashamed of the gospel of Jesus Christ.' Why? 'Because it is the power of God for the salvation of those who believe!'

The citizens of Rome were not as interested in great philosophical ideas as the Greeks were. They were interested in the more pragmatic question 'Does it work?' Paul says that 'I'm not ashamed of the gospel because it works; it is the power, the dynamite of God. It achieves something.' What does the gospel achieve? 'In the gospel the righteousness from God is revealed.' It's all about the righteousness of God. And there is an echo here of what was on Jesus' mind as he spoke to his Father, at the beginning of our story. As he prayed before his arrest and crucifixion, he refers to God not only as 'Holy Father' but as 'Righteous Father' (Jn. 17:11; 25).

From Romans 1:18 onwards, Paul unpacks the need for good news, the gospel, and he paints the dark background against which the light and truth of the message stand out. In the gospel message 'the righteousness of God is revealed' (1:17). It is about God's saving intervention, it has to do with our standing before God and it reveals that God is 'right in condemning sinners and in fulfilling his promises to provide salvation.'[24] So God is right in both judging and saving. He is a God of wrath and love simultaneously: he both judges sin and shows mercy, and each of these is a facet of his holiness.

This insight is not new to Paul, as we have seen. From the very beginning of the Bible, God has been active in judging sin. It has led to exclusion from his presence; the universal penalty of death; the destruction of humanity and the environment in the Flood and the plagues upon Egypt. The Israelites were reminded of their individual guilt every day through the sacrificial system, and of their corporate guilt every year on the Day of Atonement; and King David taught us through his experience that sin ultimately is against God himself. He takes it personally! God's wrath, as we have also seen, is always judicial; it is the wrath of a judge administering justice. It is also personal, as David reminded us, 'Against you, you only have I sinned.' Jesus spoke more of God's wrath than anyone else; telling us to 'fear him who can throw both body and soul into hell,' and warning us of the danger of being thrown into 'hell' – the place of agonising awareness of God's displeasure; the place of conscious knowledge that we have lost not only God but all good, and everything that made life seem worth living; the place of self-condemnation and self-loathing.[25]

But just as God's wrath is the universal revelation of Scripture, so are the promises of grace: from the first promise outside the Garden gate at Eden to the grace shown Noah, up to the forgiveness of David and the sufferings of the innocent Servant of the Lord. Mercy has been mixed with judgement or, to use Paul's words later in Romans, 'Note then, the kindness and severity of God' (11:22).

The gospel shows us that God is right to judge, 'For the wrath of God is revealed from heaven against all ungodliness and unrighteousness of men, who by their unrighteousness suppress the truth' (1:18 ESV). God's wrath is revealed against *ungodliness*. This comes first: no surprise to those who know Jesus' teaching. He taught that the commandments of God's law fell into two halves. The first states our duty towards God and can be summarised in these words, 'Love the Lord your God with all your heart and mind and strength.' It is our greatest sin that we do not love God as we should.

The wrath of God is also revealed against *unrighteousness*. This is the correct order; for ungodliness leads to unrighteousness. Love for God leads to love for our neighbour; the one is the test of the other. This is important: for it is possible to profess to love God while abusing or at least ignoring our neighbour. No love for God soon breaks down my relationship with my neighbour also. Ungodliness leads to unrighteousness. Whenever people abandon God or reduce their view of him, unrighteousness follows.

Paul is saying that the problem with humanity is this: we have broken both parts of the law of God, part one and part two. We don't love the Lord God with all our hearts, souls strength and minds. We disregard the truth revealed to everyone in nature and conscience. We ignore the inklings of future judgement that are universal. We turn even the knowledge of the true God into an idol of our convenience, that we make him something that suits our taste. And we treat other human beings, made in God's image, as things, sometimes worse.

How is God's wrath revealed?

That's the dark picture that Paul paints in Romans 1. And he then goes on to show how this works in practice, because he says that the wrath of God is *being* revealed against ungodliness and unrighteousness. The present tense implies a constant disclosure, going on all the time. How? Paul spells it out in words he uses three times in Romans 1, 'God gave them up.' They put a lid on the truth that they know and they suppress it. They don't glorify God as God and they never thank him for what he has done. In their thinking, they become foolish and futile, and their hearts are darkened.

> Therefore God gave them up in the lusts of their hearts to impurity, to the dishonouring of their bodies among themselves . . . God gave them up to dishonourable passions. For their women exchanged natural relations for those that are contrary to nature; and the men likewise gave up natural relations with women and were consumed with

passion for one another, men committing shameless acts with men and receiving in themselves the due penalty for their error. And since they did not see fit to acknowledge God, God gave them up to a debased mind to do what ought not to be done' (vs 24, 26–7, 28 ESV).

The wrath of God is being revealed from heaven today when he lets us do what's in our hearts to do. He says that if that's the way you want it, that's the way you'll have it. He shuts us up to the consequences of our own sinful choices. Before hell is an experience inflicted by God, it is a state for which humanity opts, by retreating from the light which God shines into our hearts to lead us to Jesus. 'And this is the judgement: the light has come into the world, and people loved darkness rather than the light because their deeds were evil' (Jn. 3:19 ESV). But there is also *wrath to come*.

But because of your hard and impenitent heart you are storing up wrath for yourself on the day of wrath when God's righteous judgement will be revealed. He will render to each one according to his works: to those who by patience in well-doing seek for glory and honour and immortality, he will give eternal life; but for those who are self-seeking and do not obey the truth, but obey unrighteousness, there will be wrath and fury (2:5–8 ESV).

How does humanity do when it is exposed to the penetrating gaze of this righteous and holy God? The apostle brings us all before the bench of God's judgement for assessment. It reaches its climax in 3:9–11 where he says, 'What then? Are we Jews any better off? No, not at all. For we have already charged that all, both Jews and Greeks, are under sin, as it is written: None is righteous, no, not one; no one understands; no one seeks for God.'

The verdict is comprehensive and conclusive. The whole world has been put on trial – rich and poor, ignorant and intelligent, people of every social rank, cultural background, religious persuasion, philosophical position, the moral and the immoral, the unrighteous and the self-righteous, the Jew and the Gentile – and the judgement has been passed. They are all *'without any exception sinful, guilty and speechless before God.'*[26] There has been not one word of mitigation, not one hint of any exception, not one suggestion of reprieve, not one sign of escape. The analysis is terrifying in its conclusion, 'None is righteous, no, not one . . . so that every mouth may be stopped, and the whole world may be held accountable to God' (Rom. 3:10,19 ESV).

'But now,' says Paul. The word 'but' indicates an immediate and definite contrast with what has gone before. 'But now,' tells us that something new and unexpected has happened. It has happened *recently*: he is emphasising the historical aspect of it all. Something has occurred in the history of humanity, a turning point has been reached. It has happened *decisively*, a new age has dawned, the turning point of history has taken place. Since humanity's fall into sin the world has been plunged into ever greater darkness; now something bright and new has come. 'But now the righteousness of God has been manifested' (3:21 ESV).

This new thing has not come out of the blue, however, because 'the Law and the Prophets bear witness to it' (3:21). This is something that the Bible has been speaking about, albeit partially, by foretellings and foreshadowings. The Law (the five books of Moses) the Prophets, particularly Isaiah, all of these have been testifying about this one thing that's happened. Now, says Paul, the righteousness from God has been revealed. We are introduced to God's grace to sinners who believe in Jesus, against the frightening background of God's judgement that declares the whole world guilty in his sight and God's wrath, which imposes the death sentence upon all humanity.

At the heart of this passage are the words 'to justify.' Whenever you read it, remember that the words to 'justify' and 'righteousness' are from the same root. Justification is a legal term, the opposite of condemnation. That sits very well in the context of Romans. The first few chapters have described the whole world in sin – the religious, moral as well as immoral world of men and women – and has found the whole lot to be under the wrath of God and condemned at the bar of his justice. We are condemned; that is the conclusion of verses 19–20. We are silenced in his courtroom; relentless guilt grips the soul of anyone who has seen themselves as God sees them. What do we need? We need to be declared right, cleared and acquitted. What is salvation? It is being 'justified;' and justification is primarily a declaration by God.

We are 'justified by his grace as a gift' (v24). Wherever we look in the New Testament, we discover that salvation was God the Father's idea. He thinks it up; he takes the initiative; he makes the moves towards us while we are still sinful, guilty and condemned, powerless and without hope. There are those who delight to try to drive a wedge between the Father and the Son. They see the references to God's wrath and try to project a Jesus who interferes with the Father's intention to judge and extracts a promise of salvation from him. But the Bible is uniform in saying that while all three members of the Trinity are involved in the plan of salvation, it is the Father who takes priority in it.

The first word to note is 'grace' itself. I do not hesitate to say that it is the greatest word in the Bible for a guilty sinner to hear. It means undeserved kindness, unmerited favour, love shown with no strings attached. It arises from the spontaneous love of God. Notice the words 'as a gift.' There is no hint of our earning it, or meriting it, or deserving it. A free gift is a free gift, period. In John's gospel the words 'as a gift,' are used by Jesus and are translated by the phrase 'without a cause;' 'they hated me without a cause' (Jn. 15:25 ESV). God has justified us by his grace 'without a cause.' He gives salvation 'freely,' 'as a gift.' It challenges our normal self-reliance. It challenges our confidence in religious activity, morality, charity, and sacrifice on behalf of others as means of getting right with God.

In this passage, grace is contrasted with works. Romans 3:21 says it comes 'apart from the law.' Some people wrongly think that God's law is like a ten-step ladder up to heaven, but the law was never intended to be that. Its *first purpose* was to show us how holy and perfect God is; and its *second purpose* was to show us how far short of God's glory we have fallen. Instead of being a ladder, the law is a mirror held up to our dirty faces and broken lives. It would be wrong to say that there was no grace in the old dispensation but it is true that in that period God's stress was upon what he required. It showed up sin in every conceivable way but there was no power to deal with it. 'But now,' something new has taken place. Now the emphasis is on the 'good news,' the gospel of our Lord Jesus Christ, and message of what God has done decisively and finally about human sin. It is the Good News message that a righteous God can put right unrighteous people.

Paul uses three metaphors to describe what God has done in order to rectify this terrible problem. What has God done about it?

The marketplace

Paul talks about redemption. The context is Romans 3:23: 'For all have sinned and fall short of the glory of God'. That is where we stand. '[We] are justified by his grace as a gift, through the redemption that is in Christ Jesus' (v24).

Of all the titles that the Christian gives to the Lord Jesus, there is none so precious as the title Redeemer. This image is drawn from the commercial realm of business transactions. The word 'redeem' means to 'buy' or 'buy back' by payment of a ransom price. It means 'deliverance at a cost' or 'release by payment' of a price.[27] In the Old Testament and in the ancient world generally this practice was widespread. Somebody paid the price necessary to free property from mortgage, animals from slaughter, and people from slavery, even death. Today, if Paul was using the imagery, he might apply it to the area of shares. Someone who has been going through a tough patch in their business might sell their shares in order to release some capital to get through the rough time. The word 'to redeem' will be used when, in better times, they can buy back their shares and re-establish their position in the firm. We find this word being used of Israel's deliverance from slavery in Egypt and exile in Babylon. In both cases, rescue and freedom were effected by a great expenditure of divine power. Christians will often talk about salvation being free but in fact it is desperately expensive. It is free at the point of delivery but only because the cost of it has been met somewhere else by Someone else.

There are two things we can learn from redemption. It obviously implies a plight from which we have been redeemed. The word 'redemption' is used in a variety of ways to illustrate what that plight is. In Ephesians 1:17

it's our 'transgression' or our sin. In Galatians 3 it's the
fact that we're under the curse of God. In 1 Peter 1:18 it's
because we're living an empty way of life that's been
handed down to us and is going nowhere. In Titus 2:14
it's all the wickedness that we accumulate in our lives,
and in Romans 8 it's the dying world that is under sin
and the dying universe that is crying out for rescue and
deliverance. Our plight is our bondage to sin, pain,
futility and decay. We need rescuing from the guilt and
condemnation of sin and the judgement and wrath of
God.

All of that is involved in redemption, the plight from
which we've been redeemed. But again the emphasis is
on the price with which we have been redeemed. The
New Testament does not press the imagery to the point of
indicating to whom the ransom was paid, but it leaves us
in no doubt about the price; it was Christ himself.
Imbedded in the word 'redemption' in the original
language (*apolutroseos*) is the little word *lutron*, 'ransom.'
In other words, the idea of redemption is deliverance or
release by payment of a ransom. In redemption,
someone's release or deliverance is accomplished at the
cost of a ransom payment. What is the ransom? What is
the payment? The word 'ransom' (*lutron*) is used only in
Mark 10:45, 'The Son of Man did not come to be served,
but to serve, and to give his life a ransom for many.' The
answer is that the life of the Son of Man is the ransom
paid in redemption. Peter also emphasises this whole
idea of a ransom price: 'You were ransomed from the
futile ways inherited from your forefathers, not with
perishable things such as silver or gold, but with the
precious blood of Christ, like that of a lamb without
blemish or spot' (1 Pet. 1:18–19).

Peter links redemption with the sacrificial lamb in
Exodus, the deliverance of the Jews from their captivity

in Egypt. We have looked at this connection earlier. He says that the real price is the precious blood of the *real* lamb, the lamb of God, Jesus Christ. He is set apart from all the other lambs. So, to quote Paul again, '[We] are justified by his grace as a gift, through the redemption that is in Christ Jesus.' He is our ransom and our peace.

The temple

Now, if Christ is our ransom, how does this ransom work? Paul uses another metaphor to explain it, this time that of the temple. The temple was the worship place. The whole issue here is what God is doing. Look again at verse 25: 'God presented him' or 'put forward' Jesus Christ. What did God do? 'Christ Jesus, whom God put forward as a propitiation by his blood, to be received by faith. This was to show God's righteousness, because in his divine forbearance he had passed over former sins. It was to show his righteousness at the present time, so that he might be just and the justifier of the one who has faith in Jesus' (Rom. 3:24b–26 ESV).

One scholar has said that in the ancient world 'religion was sacrifice'. The word 'propitation' is used here and in 1 John 2:1–2; 4:10. And some scholars have tried to change the meaning of the text here by translating it differently. There's no doubt that in pagan religions an angry god is appeased by an offering of grain or fruit. In primitive religions the god is often seen as capricious and unstable. But the background to Paul's use of this expression is undoubtedly the central act in Israel's atonement ritual.

As we have seen, the high priest was commanded to take two goats on the Day of Atonement: one was sacrificed and the other sent off into the wilderness as a scapegoat, carrying the people's sins. The blood of the goat that was sacrificed was sprinkled on the mercy seat, the cover of the Ark of the Covenant, as a means of turning away God's wrath. The point of the imagery is that sin is so serious that someone has to die for it, either the offender or an innocent substitute. The scapegoat was a lesson to the people that the death of the sacrifice had been effective and sin had been removed forever. Both these ideas are embraced in the word used here, propitiation.

The Bible makes it absolutely clear that there is no sacrifice we can bring, there's nothing we can do that can turn away God's anger. Notice the emphasis here. Who is doing the turning away of the anger? It is God himself (v25). God 'put forward' Christ as his propitiation. God did it to demonstrate his justice. God has taken the action. This is unheard of in pagan religions. Here is God in his love dealing with his own judicial wrath against our sin. He's making all the moves.

There are two parties involved in this word propitiation: the offended one and the offered one. The offended one is God. Sin arouses the wrath of God. The God of the Bible is capable of holy anger, i.e. anger without the elements of the irrational or unpredictability or malice that so often characterise our anger. The wrath of God is his steady, unrelenting, uncompromising antagonism to evil in all its forms. As John Stott says, 'God's anger is poles apart from ours. What provokes our anger (injured vanity) never provokes His; what provokes His anger (evil) seldom provokes ours.'[28]

The offered one is Christ. Unlike pagan religions, the gospel begins with the outspoken assertion that nothing we can do, say, offer or even contribute can compensate for our sins or turn away God's anger. There is no possibility of persuading, cajoling or bribing God to forgive us, for we deserve nothing at his hands but judgement. Instead the emphasis is upon God himself. God himself takes the initiative. Out of sheer love, he makes the moves to deal with his own wrath. And God himself, in the person of his Son, steps in to bear the full fury of his wrath in himself. 'God was reconciling the world to himself in Christ' (2 Cor. 5:19). This is not something that Christ is doing in order to make the Father happy, nor is it a form of cosmic 'child abuse.' Here is the Trinity in action; God is in Christ, reconciling the world to himself. Christ's work on the cross was one in which Father and Son were united in the common task of saving lost sinners, and what Christ bore, he bore without any sense of personal desert. 'He willingly bowed under the weight of a judgement whose justness only the understanding of one who was sinless could grasp fully, and he bowed under it because from eternity he had purposed to do so.'[29]

It is God the Father, in his love, who provides the very sacrifice that turns aside his righteous wrath. On the cross, the Father and Son are united in the common task of saving sinners and God in Christ dies as our substitute. Christ takes upon himself the penalty of our sin. He absorbs it and exhausts it in his own body on the tree. There is no wrath left for those who are in Christ Jesus. 'In this is love, not that we have loved God but that he loved us and sent his Son to be the propitiation for our sins. Beloved, if God so loved us, we also ought to love one another' (1 Jn. 4:10,11 ESV).

The courtroom

The third image that Paul uses is the image of the courtroom and the word 'justification'. One of the problems in our English translation is that we use several words for the same word in the original. The words 'justification', 'justifies', 'righteousness' and 'righteous' come from the same root.

Justification is a legal term and means 'to be declared to be in the right.' Justification is the opposite of condemnation. 'God presented him as a sacrifice of atonement, through faith in his blood. He did this to demonstrate his justice, because in his forbearance he had left the sins committed beforehand unpunished' (Rom. 3:25). There is a problem inherent at the very heart of Christianity, and Paul is putting his finger on it here: how can God forgive sin and remain just? We have seen that God is right in judging sinners, but the question now arises 'Is he right in saving them?'

I have said that Paul uses the language of the courtroom, and I am not the first preacher to use the illustration of the judge leaving the bench to pay the fine for the guilty offender. But of course there is no literal courtroom, and God the Judge is not the objective arbitrator of an impersonal universal law. He is Judge, offended party and Saviour. The moral law is a reflection of his holy character, and when we flout it we offend him. This is a moral universe in which God's wrath is both already known and will one day be poured out and in which he is morally bound to uphold what is right as it is reflected in the law. Rejecting the authority of God and breaking his law have unavoidable consequences; punishment is inescapable and justice must be satisfied. The whole issue is that of God himself and 'when God acts to address the outcomes of the broken moral law, he addresses these himself, himself taking the burden of his own wrath, himself absorbing in the person of Christ the judgement his righteous character cannot but demand, himself providing what no sinner can give, himself absorbing the punishment which no sinner could bear and remain in his presence.'[30]

Why did God face the problem of needing to give a public vindication of his righteousness? The answer is in the last phrase of verse 25: 'on account of passing over sins done beforehand.' For centuries God had been doing what Psalm 103:10 says; 'He does not deal with us according to our sins, nor repay us according to our iniquities' (ESV). He just passes over them. He does not punish them.

King David is a good example. As we saw in chapter 6, the prophet Nathan confronts him with his adultery with Bathsheba and the murder of her husband. Nathan says, 'Why have you despised the word of the Lord?' God asks David 'Why have you despised me?' (2 Sam. 12:9–10). David feels the rebuke of Nathan, and in verse 13 he says, 'I have sinned against the Lord.' To this, Nathan responds, 'The LORD has taken away your sin. You are not going to die.' Just like that! Adultery and murder are passed over. That is what Paul means in Romans 3:25 by the passing over of sins done beforehand. Animal sacrifices were not enough to deal with sin. Yet God forgave people their sin then. How could he do it? Because the people of the Old Testament believed his promise and thereby looked to Christ. They did not see things clearly, but they believed the promise, they made their offerings by faith, they looked forward to the perfect sacrifice and in faith they held to it. In other words, from the very beginning that had been been God's plan to send his Son to be our Saviour, so that the effects of his death would work backwards as well as forwards.

On the Cross on Calvary's hill God was giving a public explanation of what He had been doing throughout the centuries. By so doing, and at the same time, He vindicates His own eternal character of righteousness and of holiness.[31]

How has God vindicated himself? He has poured out on his only begotten and beloved Son his wrath upon sin.

Propitiation

John Owen said that propitiation has four necessary elements: first, an offence to be taken away; second, a person offended who needs to be pacified; third, an offending person; and fourth, a sacrifice to make atonement for the offence. The opposition to this teaching again comes from those who reject any idea of God's wrath and see it as inconsistent with the revelation of his love. Yet it is God himself, the offended party, who initiates the action that will appease his wrath and turn away his anger by dealing with his offended justice. That is the reason for the cross. God the Father is behind it. It is all of God from first to last. God's wrath is no fit of spite. It is not his emotional response to our bad behaviour. It is his settled opposition to all that is evil, arising out of his very nature. It is because 'God is light and in him is no darkness at all' (1 Jn.1) that he is in settled opposition to everything that is evil. His nature is that he abhors evil, he hates evil.[32] Wrath is the inevitable consequence of sin. Yet Christ is put forward as a propitiation. God acts to deal with his own moral and judicial demands by taking our sin on himself in Christ and bearing the penalty our sin demands.

God purposed Jesus Christ to be a propitiatory sacrifice in order that 'he might justify sinners righteously, that is, in a way that is altogether worthy of himself as the truly loving and merciful eternal God.' For God to have forgiven their sin lightly would have been 'to have compromised with the lie that moral evil does not matter and so to have violated his own truth and mocked men with an empty, lying reassurance, which, at their most human, they must have recognized as the squalid falsehood which it would have been.'[33] This was the only way for him to vindicate himself as 'just and the justifier of the one who has faith in Jesus.'

Here is the justification of God, and there's the justification of believers. It's not as if God simply rates us as righteous although we really aren't. That would be a legal fiction. Nor is it simply that he makes us righteous in a moral sense, for we are manifestly not. Nor does he pronounce us not sinners. That would be a lie. No, he pronounces that we are not guilty; that is, without legal liability. Why? Because the law's demands have been met by Christ, as our sin is credited to his account and his righteousness is credited to ours. We call this 'imputation'. My sins are imputed to Christ: his righteousness is imputed to me. All charges are therefore dropped, and the verdict that we would normally expect to be pronounced on the Day of Judgement is pronounced now whenever someone trusts in Jesus. This is what Paul argues in Romans 8:1 'There is now no condemnation for those who are in Christ Jesus.' This legal transaction takes place, what Athanasius calls the 'amazing exchange'. All the merit of Christ is given to me. God is justified, I am justified, so God is demonstrated to be 'just and the justifier of the one who has faith in Jesus.' All of this comes from God's grace. We are justified freely by his grace.

Earlier I mentioned the connection between the mercy seat and propitiation. Whenever the blood was sprinkled on the mercy seat it was sign that the sacrifice was made and the wrath turned away. Sin was dealt with and people were thereby cleared of sin and guilt: they were 'mercy-seated.'

Jesus tells about two men who went to pray. One was a Pharisee and one was a tax collector. The religious man obviously thought he was very important and prayed to God in very important language. The tax collector couldn't even lift up his eyes and said 'God, be merciful to me, a sinner.' Do you know what he literally said? 'God be mercy-seated to me, a sinner.' Jesus said the man who prayed that prayer went home justified.

Act 3 Scene 2

The great exchange

We have been watching the drama of redemption unfold through history, climaxing in the work of Christ on the cross. The question is: what next? And the answer to that is the church, the people the Father has given to the Son (to use the language Jesus uses in John 17) and their great task in the world. What is the church to do with this message committed to it by Jesus? What is our part in the drama of redemption?

The importance of evangelism

What is the church in the world for? It is one of the questions that often entertain those whose job is to galvanise the Christian public into some kind of activity – diverting their money into good causes or coming up with some kind of action plan for the next five years. What in the world is the church for or what is the church in the world for? Archbishop William Temple put it like this: 'The church is the only society that exists for the benefit of the non-members.' Emil Brunner said that 'the church exists by mission as a fire exists by burning.'

When we look at the New Testament and especially the book of Acts, we discover that while we say that we *believe* in evangelism, the early church actually *did* it. It was launched into the world by the Spirit on the Day of Pentecost. From a handful of people at the beginning, within ten years it had reached Alexandria and Antioch, the greatest cities in Africa and Asia respectively. It had already arrived in Rome, the capital of the world and by the end of the first century had reached a multiplicity of races and cultures and penetrated into every class of society. People were becoming Christians, sometimes in large numbers, sometime one by one. Yet evangelism easily slips down the agenda of our churches today. Yes, we hold courses on it, we get speakers to talk about it and our major church bodies devise strategies and schemes. We talk a lot about it but our practice contradicts our words. Most of our energies as Christian groups are being poured into entertaining bored Christian young people, comforting old Christians, sharing Christian charity or maintaining Christian institutions. If you doubt that, do a survey of what occupies the time of most Christian professionals – those in any kind of paid ministry position, and it will shock you. Very little in real terms is invested in evangelism, getting the gospel out there.

This contradicts what we see in the Bible. What do we see in the New Testament? Obviously there's the role of the evangelist – those who are called especially to go and evangelise among the people. But what we also find in the New Testament is this: Christian pastors are told to do the work of an evangelist and Christian believers are told always to be ready to give an answer to anyone who asks for a reason for the hope that they have. And

Christian churches are commended, as the Philippians are, for standing together as one man for the sake of the gospel: the business of getting the gospel out to the world. So what is evangelism?

Back in 1974 the Lausanne Covenant described evangelism like this: 'Evangelism is the proclamation of the historical, biblical Christ as Saviour and Lord, with a view to persuading people to come to him personally and so be reconciled to God.'

What does evangelism involve?

What does the work of evangelism require? Paul in 2 Corinthians is talking about his ministry, and part of this ministry is getting the gospel out. Paul argues that the work of evangelism requires both personal and biblical integrity. 'Therefore, since through God's mercy we have this ministry, we do not lose heart. Rather, we have renounced secret and shameful ways; we do not use deception, nor do we distort the word of God' (2 Cor. 4:1,2). The work of evangelism requires us to be always above board in what we are doing; not be manipulative or use subtleties, nor taking advantages of people's weaknesses, but always being straight about what we're doing and why. 'Nor do we distort the word of God': it is absolutely vital that we tell people what the Bible says and not what we would like it to say. We can neither leave out the bits we find uncomfortable nor modify the claims of Christ: we must say it like it is.

The apostle uses the word 'ambassador' to describe his task (2 Cor. 5:20). Paul is an Apostle, and there are many things that he says in this letter that are unique to his office. But although there is a unique and primary application of the word 'ambassador' to Paul as an apostle, there is a general application to ourselves. 'We are therefore Christ's ambassadors.' An evangelist is an 'ambassador' – a representative of another country and another king. It highlights our 'alien' status here. We are 'in the world but not of the world.' When I was living in North America, my legal status was that of residential alien. Whenever I went into Canada and back again, I always had to follow the sign that said 'Aliens this way!' This is not a new idea. In our first text, Jesus distinguishes his people from the world in which they live: 'they are not of the world any more than I am of the world' (Jn. 17:14). In Philippians, Paul reminds us that we are aliens and strangers here. The writer to the Hebrews is constantly telling us that we don't have any abiding city; we are looking to another city, the heavenly Jerusalem. Here we are pilgrims and ambassadors of another country and another king: Jesus.

The role of ambassador is also one of great dignity when it is someone who represents a great power. It is an even greater dignity for the Christian who represents King Jesus. Charles Simeon was one of the great Anglican preachers of his age, and he wrote to a young man called John Venn who was being ordained into the Anglican ministry, on the occasion of his ordination in 1782. This is what he writes in his card

> I most sincerely congratulate you not on a permission to receive £40 or £50 a year, nor on the title of Reverend, but on your accession to the most valuable, most honourable, most important, and most glorious office in the world – to that of an ambassador of the Lord Jesus Christ.

To be an ambassador means to be a representative or an envoy and to be a spokesperson. An ambassador 'does not speak in his own name. He does not act on his own authority. What he communicates is not his own opinions or demands, but simply what he has been told to say; that's why we don't distort the Word of God. At the same time he speaks with authority, in this case the authority of Christ.'[34]

Persuasion

'Therefore, knowing the fear of the Lord, we persuade others' (5:11 ESV). The word 'persuasion' is not just a rational activity of trying to muster arguments; it also has an element of emotion in it. Luke uses various words in Acts to describe it: to teach, argue, dispute, prove – all of these words have both reason and emotion involved in them. In evangelism, we are not simply involving ourselves in cool communication, but seeking actively to get at the minds and hearts of people to persuade them that Christ is the only Saviour of the world, that hell is as real as heaven, and that people must trust in Christ alone for salvation.

Passion

'Therefore, we are ambassadors for Christ, God making his appeal through us. We implore you on behalf of Christ, be reconciled to God' (5:20 ESV). Again, this is a blend of reason and emotion. There are reasons why we implore people – 'You need to be reconciled to God, you need to be put right with God.' There are eternal issues at stake. We may say, 'Understand that with your mind, but it is imperative that you make the right choice. I want you to understand what Jesus has done on the cross and what that involves, but at the same time, if I could do anything to persuade you, to take you to one side and shake you, if that would get through to you the need for a Saviour and the absolute, priority of trusting in Christ, then I would do it.'

Why? God is making his appeal through us. Elsewhere Paul says that we become fools and make ourselves vulnerable in order that we may fulfil our ministry and persuade people to come to Christ. Its part of our increasing commitment to Christ that we will feel what he feels for a perishing world and our hearts will burn with a passion that speaks on Christ's behalf.

What are we up against?

Why has evangelism slipped off the radar of people's thinking? The answer is this: evangelism is hard. Even the apostle Paul knew this. Twice in chapter 4 Paul talks about 'losing heart'; 'We do not lose heart' (4:1 ESV) and 'Therefore we do not lose heart' (4:16 ESV) Why is Paul saying this twice in the space of this little section? Because he's saying, 'Even I am tempted to lose heart. It's hard work and there's all kind of discouragements. People aren't gagging for you to tell them about God, Christ, Heaven and Hell.'

We are up against spiritual blindness: 'the god of this world has blinded the minds of the unbelievers, to keep them from seeing the light of the gospel of the glory of Christ, who is the image of God' (4:4 ESV). There is this spiritual battle going on. When I speak to someone of Christ, there are spiritual forces at work that are trying to destroy every word I say. The devil is aiding people's own radical unbelief, all the time giving people reasons not to believe. That's why evangelism is hard. People are unbelievers and there is something intentional about their unbelief. It's not just that they don't believe and they're on neutral ground and somehow we need to help them move from their neutrality. They are negative, determined in their unbelief. Satan is the enemy of the gospel and the enemy of people's souls. So he sets about trying to distort the gospel. In every age we have to clarify and defend it.

We are also up against our own personal weakness: 'But we have this treasure (this immense message of salvation) in jars of clay' (4:7 ESV). 'Jars of clay' were the most basic of household items, simple and fragile, worth little and easily shattered. Paul is saying, 'We are ordinary people with ordinary people's vulnerabilities.'[35] We have faults and failings. If anyone was ever tempted to give up, Paul was, as he goes through all the things that he describes in the verses that follow. He had been challenged emotionally, psychologically, spiritually, and he's been through tiredness, pain and suffering. He understood what it was to be a simple jar of clay. Evangelism has slipped off the agenda because it's hard, and it's hard because of spiritual blindness and personal weakness.

Please don't misunderstand what I am saying. Confessing evangelicals are committed to acts of mercy, that is to social action and caring for people on a practical level, but church history shows how easily the balance can swing away from gospel work to social work. Acts of mercy and charity are part and parcel of our general Christian responsibility to our neighbours and even our enemies. But the church on earth is 'the pillar and buttress of truth' (1 Tim. 3:15) charged with defining, declaring and defending the gospel.

Why bother?

The fear of God

'Therefore, knowing the fear of the Lord, we persuade others' (5:11 ESV). I wonder whether we know what it is to fear God. The previous verse tells us why Paul fears God: 'For we must all appear before the judgement seat of Christ, so that each one may receive what is due for what he has done in the body, whether good or evil. Therefore, knowing the fear of the Lord, we persuade others' (5:10, 11 ESV).

Do you see the connection? It is judgement. We all know that there is judgement to come for sinners. On that day of judgement, God will underline the decision that sinners have made and will shut them up to the consequences of their actions: there will be no one in hell who hasn't chosen to be there. That's the final judgement but Paul isn't talking about that. Notice he says, 'We'. He is speaking to believers here. 'We must all appear before the judgement seat of Christ.' Christian people are particularly conscious of that day. We have been given much – by way of spiritual understanding, gifts and opportunities for service – and from those to whom much is given, much shall be required. This is not meant 'to cloud the believer's prospect of future blessedness, but to act as a stimulus.'[36] The way we conduct our lives here should constantly be influenced by the thought that everything is naked and open before the eyes of the One with whom we have to do. Every secret is open to him, whose gaze penetrates beyond what is on the surface of our lives. He sees to the very essence of our personality.

The effect of this fear of God will be twofold. It will make us *urgent*. We will not waste our time but will buy up every opportunity. As Paul says, 'In the presence of

God and of Christ Jesus, who will judge the living and the dead, and in view of his appearing and his kingdom, I give you this charge: Preach the Word' (2 Tim. 4:1, 2). It will make us *consistent*. 'What we are is plain to God, and I hope it is also plain to your conscience' (2 Cor. 5:11b). Every preacher and every Christian witness has to preach and share the word in view of the judgement seat of Christ.

Paul is so conscious of this when he speaks to the Ephesian elders, and after three years of being with them he says, 'I have not held back from you anything that would have done you good. I have preached to you the whole counsel of God, and I've done in light of the fact that we who teach will be judged all the more severely on that day.' If we take the judgement seat of Christ seriously, it will make us urgent in the work that we do.

The Son of God

'For Christ's love compels us, because we are convinced that one died for all, and therefore all died' (2 Cor. 5:14 ESV). The great compelling motive in Paul's life since his conversion is love. But this love is not something that begins and ends in himself; rather it begins and ends with God in Christ. The Greek verb used here is used in the gospels, and especially by Luke, of the crowds thronging Jesus, pressing in to be near him, to touch him. It is used also of armies surrounding Jerusalem and 'hemming it in on every side'. Luke also uses it in medical contexts of people who were 'gripped' by fever, or by a powerful emotion like fear or distress. In each case there is a strong pressure, physical or psychological, which grasps hold of a person, and controls or compels them. Now the pressure Paul feels is the love of God in Christ. This love was not simply a warm glow in his stomach but a fire in his heart lit by these massive convictions.

Firstly, he says 'one has died for all' (2 Cor. 5:14 ESV). All were sinners, all deserved to die because the wages of sin is death. But only one died instead of them, on their behalf, in their place. Crucifixion was the death of the curse, since God had said, 'Cursed is everyone who is hung on a tree' but Paul had come to see that Jesus had taken up the curse of the punishment of sin in the place of his people. He wrote to the Romans, 'But God demonstrates his own love for us in this: While we were still sinners, Christ died for us' (Rom. 5:8). And again to the Galatians, 'Christ redeemed us from the curse of the law by becoming a curse for us' (Gal. 3:13). Second, 'One has died for all, therefore all have died': we were there when they crucified our Lord. He died as our substitute and sin bearer therefore we are considered to have died in him. His death was our death. Third, 'He died for all, that those who live might no longer live for themselves but for him who for their sake died and was raised.' He died and rose for us that we might live for him. This is the irresistible logic of the love of Christ. We owe our life to his love and this leaves us with no option. John Stott once wrote

> Nothing shuts the mouth, seals the lips, and ties the tongue, like the poverty of our own spiritual experience. We do not bear witness for the simple reason that we have no witness to bear.[37]

Paul gives his own testimony, 'From now on, therefore, we regard no one according to the flesh. Even though we once regarded Christ according to the flesh, we regard him thus no longer.' Why? 'If anyone is in Christ, he is a new creation. The old has passed away; behold, the new has come!' (5:16, 17 ESV). We get on with the work of evangelism because Jesus has made such a difference to

us and we believe that Jesus Christ can save the most
unlikely people. We don't give up on anyone, because
God doesn't give up on anyone.

Do we believe the gospel?

Paul has spoken about the fear of God and the Son of God
as the driving forces of his life but he has one other, the
gospel of God. We will only be committed to evangelism if
we believe in the gospel. I think that those who have lost
confidence in evangelism have done so because they've
lost confidence in the evangel, the gospel. 'All this is from
God, who reconciled us to himself through Christ and
gave us the ministry of reconciliation: that God was
reconciling the world to himself in Christ, not counting
men's sins against them' (5:18, 19). The gospel is the story
of God's action in Christ. The heart of the gospel is
reconciliation. Reconciliation presupposes alienation and
alienation works in both ways. I am alienated from God
because he irritates me, annoys me; and I'm allergic to
him. When he intrudes into my life and tells me what to
do, I feel I want to tell him to get lost. Our part is to be
reconciled to God. But the real problem is that God is
alienated from me. He is hostile to me and is my enemy
at one level, and the question is 'Can God be reconciled to
us?'

The gospel has the answer; he can be reconciled to us,
at great cost in one past and decisive event: 'God made
him who had no sin to be sin for us, so that in him we
might become the righteousness of God' (2 Cor. 5:21).
Earlier he said, 'All this is from God, who reconciled us to
himself through Christ.' The tense of the word
'reconciled' denotes something that has happened once
and for all in the past. The scholars say that the full force
must be given to it. 'Reconciliation is not something that

is being done, it is something that has been done, it is something that has been finished,' writes Professor Denny.

This reconciliation involves three actions. First, God chose not to count our sins against us. We deserve to be punished for them. The psalmist says, 'If you kept a record of sins, who could stand?' Then, God takes our sins and counts them against Jesus; 'For our sake he made him to be sin who knew no sin.' Remember here that Jesus is not a third party; for 'God was reconciling the world to himself in Christ' (5:19); this is God in action. Jesus understood it like this: 'it is the Father, living in me, who is doing his work' (Jn. 14:10b). Christ is not only the focus of divine revelation; he is also the means of divine redemption. There is complete identity of action between the redemptive action of Christ and that of God, though it is the Father who takes the initiative. Christ is the sinless one: as a human being, he was free of sin throughout his life on earth. On the cross, however, he was 'made sin for us.' This takes us to the heart of the atonement and one of the most profound mysteries in the universe. All the interpretations of this phrase have the idea of God causing his Son to be completely identified with something that was foreign to his experience, namely human sin. The Father's set purpose was matched by the Son's firm resolution to go to the cross in our place to bear the penalty due to us (Mk. 8:31; Lk. 9:51).

Finally, God credits his Son's righteousness to our account; 'so that in him we might become the righteousness of God' (2 Cor. 5:21). He chooses not to hold our sin against us. He takes our sin and holds Jesus responsible for it. He then takes his righteousness and credits it to our account. He pays our debts, you get his Visa card! 'As a result of the reconciliation achieved by Christ's becoming sin (v21), God no longer debits believers' accounts with a listing of their trespasses.'[38] In the Bible, forgiveness means that God chooses not to reckon our sins against us. But it also means a crediting to us of Christ's perfect righteousness. Christ gets something that is alien to him, namely our sin, while we get from him something that is alien to us, namely his righteousness. At the heart of the gospel there is this glorious exchange. Listen to what Martin Luther says: 'Lord Jesus, you are my righteousness, I am your sin. You took on you what was mine, yet set upon me what was yours. You became what you were not, that I might become what I was not.' That's the heart of the good news of the gospel, of what God has done in Christ.

In *The Lion, the Witch and the Wardrobe*,[39] Edmund traitorously joins the witch's side and the other children ally themselves with the Narnians faithful to Aslan the King. The climax of the story comes when the witch claims the right to slay Edmund for his treachery in betraying his siblings. Aslan then offers his life for Edmund's, an exchange that will free Edmund but result in Aslan's death. Lucy and Susan witness the horrific shaving of Aslan's mane and his death on the Stone Table. The Table cracks, and while they grieve for him, Aslan returns, resurrected from the dead. He tells them that what has happened resulted from a 'Deeper Magic from before the dawn of Time' which held that if an innocent victim who had committed no crime takes the place of a traitor, the Table will crack and Death will work backwards.

The great drama of redemption is being played out today as Christian people proclaim this story to the world and implore people to be reconciled to this amazing God who has acted so lovingly on our behalf.

Act 3 Scene 3

God is love

We have been exploring the drama of redemption through the lens of Jesus' prayer before his arrest on the night before his death. Much of what we have discovered so far reflects on our view of God. Is God a God of wrath as well as mercy? Is God a God of love and of judgement?

A friend of mine was giving a lecture at a well known seminary about God. One student, let's call him Bill, responded politely but firmly that he liked to think of God rather differently. For several minutes, Bill painted a picture of a friendly deity. He liked to think of God as wise but not meddling; compassionate, but never over-powering; ever so resourceful, but never interrupting. 'This,' said Bill in conclusion, 'is how I like to think of God.' My friend's reply was sharp but to the point. 'Thank you, Bill,' he said, 'for telling us so much about yourself, but we are concerned to know what God is really like.'[40]

The real issue that stands between non-Christian and Christian and between orthodox and unbiblical Christian thinking is our view of God. Certainly this is true in the current discussion about the nature of the gospel. Christians who hold to a liberal theology tend to use the Bible as a kind of supermarket; surveying its shelves and then randomly selecting a phrase or expression that provides them with some clue to the 'real' message of Jesus. Once we examine such selections, it becomes apparent that their discovery, far from being the earth-shattering new idea they claim it to be, is only another tired rehashing of old heresies. One favourite is the expression in 1 John that 'God is love.' One recent writer considers it a tragedy that Church history has obscured the centrality of God's love. He asserts that the Bible 'never defines God as anger, power or judgement – in fact it never defines him as anything other than love'. Moreover, he argues, to think of God's attributes without reference to the primary lens of his love 'is to risk a terrible misrepresentation of his character, which in turn leads to a distortion of the gospel'.[41]

The question is: is he right? To find the answer, we need to go to the very book where the expression 'God is love' is found. There are two expressions used of God here in 1 John. The first is that God is light and the second is that God is love. We are not free to pick and choose from these two expressions but must see them in their context.

Let us put them in context first of all. John is writing a letter. What is John's big idea? The opening verses are helpful, as we would expect. They define the big idea of the book as being 'fellowship'. We have fellowship with *God* – as we trust in his Son. We have fellowship with *the apostles* – as we accept their witness to Jesus. And we have fellowship with *other believers* – he says that you only really have fellowship with each other if you love one another.

John focuses first of all on the fellowship there is with God himself through the work of Jesus Christ.

Apparently there were people questioning this, claiming that it was possible to have life and fellowship with the Father without Jesus playing any significant part. It was some form of Christless religion.[42] John replies by emphasising that Christian fellowship is with the Father and the Son, and later on he will make it abundantly clear that nobody can enjoy a relationship with God without a relationship with Jesus (1 Jn. 2:23). At the same time, he stresses that eternal life is found only in Jesus. This is at once the most surprising and most reassuring thing in the world. It is surprising because we are not naturally in fellowship with God. It is the unique blessing of the Christian to find ourselves in fellowship with God. The issue that threatens our fellowship with God is ultimately who and what God himself is. This leads him to start in this unconventional way: 'This is the message we have heard from him and declare to you: God is light; in him there is no darkness at all' (1 Jn. 1:5).

He then goes on from verse 6 onwards to say this: there is darkness in us and he describes it in a whole variety of ways. We can only have fellowship with God if there is no darkness in us. The biggest threat to our relationship with God is God himself.

God is light

John starts with the message of Jesus. 'This is the message we have heard from him and declare to you,' he writes. He has just given us his credentials as an eyewitness of Jesus' life and ministry. He says, 'We were with him from the beginning, we heard him, we looked at him, we saw him, we even touched him, the word of life.' He is stating that he heard this message from Jesus himself and that at the heart of it was this assertion: 'God is light.' This is one of a variety of descriptions we have of God in the Bible. God is described as spirit (Jn. 4:24). Moreover, both Testaments affirm that God is a 'consuming fire' (Deut. 4:24; Heb. 12:29), and dwells in 'unapproachable light' (1 Tim. 6:16).

The whole idea of light conveys two ideas: revelation and perfection. Truth and righteousness are all embraced in this idea of light. The very first thing we find God saying in Genesis 1 is 'Let there be light' and there was. God has let his light shine because there is nothing he needs to hide. God has made himself seen in his absolute purity and unutterable majesty. Throughout Scripture, God divides light from darkness, and overcomes darkness by light. The appearances of God to people are always accompanied by a great light, sometimes described as his 'glory.'

Metaphorically, the contrast between light and darkness is that between truth and error, good and evil, righteousness and wickedness (Ps. 36:9; 37:6 43:3; 119:130; Prov. 4:18; 6:23; 13:9). In sin, we are in darkness, but in Christ we are light (Eph. 5:8). The church's great task is to turn people 'from darkness to light' (Acts 26:18). You will notice that the effect of God's being light is to highlight our sin. The sight of God's holiness filled Isaiah with dread and made him conscious of his guilt (Is.6:1–5). A miracle by Jesus led Peter to cry out, 'Get away from me Lord, for I am a sinful man.' Jesus' coming is described as a revelation of light and he called himself 'the light of the world' (Mt. 4:16; Lk. 2:32; Jn. 1:4–9; 3:19–21; 8:12; 9:5). If Jesus didn't use the expression, he certainly laid the foundation for it. In the Sermon on the Mount, for example, he tells us to 'be perfect' as our Father in heaven is perfect. He cranks up the pressure when he explains that God's commands relate not simply to outward actions like murder but to inward attitudes like anger.

This view of God completely transforms the way we look at religion. Religious experience is understood by many as a means of self-fulfillment – what the individual gets out of it – not whether there is 'another' who is 'outer' and 'other' than ourselves. Religion is domesticated, trivialised, and simply co-opted for personal and private use. It is what sociologist Os Guinness describes as a faith that is 'privately engaging but socially irrelevant.'[43]

Yet there is One who stands outside and above, proclaiming 'I am who I am' (Ex. 3:14). His voice disturbs us because he does not speak the language of the market, nor of this world. Rather, he calls us to lay everything at his feet and to worship him because he is who he is, the *Holy Other.* This is the God we see in the Scriptures, and it is the Christ we encounter in the gospels.

So John starts with God. He hardly waits for an introduction. He doesn't presume that Christian people will invariably have right thoughts of God. He says, 'This is the message we have heard from him [Jesus] and declare to you: God is light' (1 Jn. 1:5). There you have the difference between liberal and biblical theology. Liberal theology always puts man in the centre. Biblical theology always puts God at the centre. New movements often put humanity at the centre and say that it should drive the way we do church and express the gospel. Biblical theology puts God in the centre and says that God should drive the way we think about church and Christianity.

John starts with God and in particular with the holiness of God. Everything that follows demonstrates that God is ethically pure and that his blinding holiness highlights our human distance from him. To live in the light we must live free from sin. To live in the darkness is to live in sin. We cannot have fellowship with God if we choose to live in darkness.

What does living in the darkness look like? He goes on to say that we are living in the darkness if we will not confess our sin to God (1 Jn. 1:6, 8) or if we refuse to keep his commands (1 Jn. 2:1–6). We are living in the darkness if we hate our Christian brother or sister (1 Jn. 2:9–11), if we love the world and the things of the world (1 Jn. 2:15–17) or reject orthodox Christian teaching about the Father and the Son (1 Jn. 2:18–25). We are walking in darkness if we make a practice of sinning (1 Jn. 3:4–10), or deny the message of Christ's apostles (1 Jn. 4:1–6). We are living in darkness if we do not love other Christians (1 Jn. 4:7–21).

What are we to do? The first move out of darkness is to confess our sin. 'If we claim to be without sin, we deceive ourselves and the truth is not in us. If we confess our sins, he is faithful and just and will forgive us our sins and purify us from all unrighteousness' (1 Jn. 1:8, 9). Now there is a strange form of words used here. We might have expected it to say that God is 'faithful' and merciful or gracious or even loving, but instead John says that 'God is faithful and *just* to forgive us our sins.' How could God be 'just' in forgiving my sin? The answer is in the next chapter, 'But if anyone does sin, we have an advocate with the Father, Jesus Christ, the Righteous.' He is the atoning sacrifice for our sins, and not only for ours but also for the sins of the whole world.

Our relationship with God begins when we step out of the shadows into the light, when we move away from the darkness and come into God's presence and we say to God, 'Dear God, I am a sinner and I need your pardon.' That's how we begin the Christian life, by admitting that we're not right. That's why being a hypocrite is the direct opposite of being a Christian, because a Christian has to stand in the presence of God and say, 'I am a sinner.'

God is love

If you are coming to this statement for the first time you might be surprised to see how almost incidental it is to the flow of the apostle's argument. He is not here writing about God primarily but about us. He is working out the doctrine he has been giving up to 4:6. There are good reasons for believing that he has nothing new to say by way of teaching beyond that point and he is moving to apply and reinforce what has been taught up to this point. So in explaining what it means to walk in darkness, he had listed 'hating' our brothers and sisters in Christ. The positive way of describing our response to our Christian family is to say we should 'love one another' (1 Jn. 4:7–21). Secondly, he had talked about the need to keep the commands of Jesus (1 Jn. 5:1–5). And third, he had taught about the saving value of having right doctrine. Wrong doctrine leads to death (1 Jn. 5:6–12).

From 4:7 the apostle John is dealing once again with the importance of brotherly love. 'Love one another' was one of the last commands Jesus gave his disciples. The world will oppose the people of God. Christian people will often experience trouble, but the thing that will convince the world that we are followers of Jesus is this: 'that you love one another.' One of the last things Jesus said before he went home to heaven was, 'Love one another.' This is the ultimate test of our profession of the Christian faith. Orthodoxy is essential, and John takes time to stress that. But it is not the ultimate test since it is perfectly possible for a person to be correct and yet not be a Christian. Christian conduct is also essential as a test of our reality. But even here it is possible to live a moral, ethically upstanding life and not to be a Christian. The ultimate test is love. And he is not talking about love in general but about love between Christian people. It is taking the words of 1 Corinthians 13 and applying them to people in Christ whom we like and whom we dislike. Christians are not perfect and yet our expectations of one another are enormous. Hence we get disappointed in one another more easily. But love involves us detaching ourselves from the problem we have with another person, looking at it not as it affects us but as Christ sees it.

He has urged love upon us before in this letter. Love is evidence that we are 'in the light' (1 Jn. 2:8,10). Love is evidence that we have 'eternal life' (1 Jn. 3:14–15). How does he begin? 'Let us love one another,' he says. Loving one another is evidence that you don't walk in the darkness any more, evidence that you are a Christian. If you said to John, 'OK, I've got the doctrines right and I'm obeying the commands of Jesus but I don't love my brothers and sisters in Christ', John would have said that that third thing cancels out the other two.

God's eternal nature

Notice the poet in John. He has a very different kind of personality and temperament to the apostle Paul, for example. Paul would have started out with his conclusion and then worked it out. John builds up to his point. He says that we should love one another because that's what happens when people have been 'born of God' and know God. Then he uses a negative statement: 'Anyone who does not love does not know God, because God is love.' Dr Lloyd-Jones says

> John does not say merely that God loves us or that God is loving. He goes beyond that. He says, 'God is love; God

essentially is love; God's nature is love; you cannot think of God without love.[44]

Saint Augustine thought that this helps us understand the doctrine of the Trinity. God has always loved and has always had an object of love within himself. God, being God, by definition is beyond understanding, but in so far as he has revealed himself in the Bible, God is one God in three persons: Father, Son and Holy Spirit. And when it says 'God is love' – that is the nature of God – it's saying that God has always been love. Subtract from your imagination everything that you can see and touch and taste, the stars and the galaxies and the planets, people and angels and archangels and cherubim and so on. Subtract everything so that all that's left is God. That's what there was at the beginning. There was just God and God was love then. This takes us back where we started in John 17, overhearing that conversation between the Lord Jesus on earth and his Father in heaven. 'Father, I want you to give me back the glory I had with you before the world existed.' And then at the end of the conversation he is praying for his people and he says, in my paraphrase, 'Father, I want those people that you have given to me, to be with me where I am, to see my glory and to share the love that you always had for me and I always had for you.'

Before there was anything there was love, for the Father always loved the Son and the Son always loved the Father, and there was always a relationship of love. The glorious thing about the Christian life is that it is your destiny to share that love relationship with the Father and the Son for all eternity; to share it as adopted sons and daughters of God. His eternal nature is to love. When we use the word 'love' we have to redefine it. The word is sung to us daily and we hear it in our plays and films and often its meaning is obscured or else debased.

We need to hold this statement together with all the other statements about God. He is light and life and fire and spirit and he is faithful and just as well. So although he is love, he does not overlook or condone sin. Rather, 'his love has found a way to expose it (because he is light) and to consume it (because he is fire) without destroying the sinner, but rather saving him.'[45] How does God's love manifest itself?

God's gracious activity

The God who is love 'loved us and sent his Son as an atoning sacrifice for our sins' (1 Jn. 4:10). The coming of Christ is a concrete historical revelation of God's love. It teaches us that, at its heart, love is self-sacrificial. There can be no suggestion of the pagan idea of a sacrificial death which extracts from God (or the god) something which he is unwilling to give. No, it is God who is loving us and sacrificing himself for us in Christ. In giving us his Son he is giving us the greatest gift possible. He gives his Son to deal with our sins. There is costly self-sacrifice involved and there is something else. There is a dealing with sin through 'propitiation.' We have already seen that that word means a sacrifice that turns away wrath, that pacifies righteous anger.

One writer speaks for the new kind of evangelical when he asks how we have 'come to believe that at the cross this God of love suddenly decides to vent his anger and wrath on his own Son?'[46] He considers this to be a mockery of Jesus' teaching about refusing to repay evil with evil and a contradiction of the statement that God is love. He insists that the cross isn't 'a form of cosmic child abuse – a vengeful Father, punishing his Son for an offence he has not even committed'. Instead the cross is a symbol of love, a demonstration of how far God is willing to go to prove his love.[47]

My question is 'Who said the cross is as he suggests?' The penal substitution view of the atonement, taught as we have seen throughout the Bible, is about a gracious God acting to deal with the consequences of our sin – the wrath and judgement we deserve. People will often ask after some disaster or tragedy, 'How could a God of love allow this or that?' It is a question often wrung out of a broken or breaking heart. Sometimes it is a smokescreen to avoid the implications of the gospel. But whatever the reason, it begs the question, why should people think that God is love? Where else in human religion is that thought to be found? Even within Christianity, what convinced the early Christians to believe that God is love?

The answer is straightforward: it is the cross. 'But God demonstrates his own love for us in this: While we were still sinners, Christ died for us' (Rom. 5:8). How do we know that God is a God of love? How can we be sure that he will forgive our sins? In particular, picking up that strange language we noticed at the beginning of this book, how can God be both 'faithful and *just*' to forgive us our sins? (1 Jn.1:9).

God's love is manifested in what he has done for guilty sinners. It is demonstrated in his activity towards rebels, people who have abused their own humanity; resisted his will, who regularly live as if he had no prior claim upon them. We don't appreciate God's love because we don't really see what insignificant creatures we are; what unworthy sinners we are, what guilty rebels we are, how deserving of hell and judgement we are. We are in fact far from being lovable or loving. By nature we hate the God who is there. That is not to say we hate the idea of God, just that we find fault in the God who has revealed himself in Christ, he is not at all what we want. We may want bits of him but we want to select for ourselves what bits those are.

We see this in the popular theory of the love of God held by people in the West which has no regard for the God of matchless holiness described in both the Old Testament and New Testament. We do not like to think that our state of sin runs so deep that it took the death of God's Son to make it possible for him to be 'faithful and *just*' to forgive us our sin. Sin is such a trifle to us we cannot understand what a big deal it is to God. This merely serves to highlight the rebelliousness of our hearts. We don't appreciate God's love because we don't see the lengths to which he is prepared to go for us.

In the first week of January 2006 many of us watched with keen interest as the tragic events unfolded at the Sago mine in West Virginia. At the time a friend wrote this comment

> Miner family member John Casto has been widely reported as saying that after the first report (twelve miners were alive), people at Sago Baptist Church 'were praising God,' but after the second report (twelve miners were dead), 'they were cursing.' One television report was more explicit about the cursing. Apparently, when the worst of all news had come, the pastor of the church told people to keep looking to God. But one man shouted, 'What in hell has God ever done for us?'[48]

The answer, of course, is that in Christ, God himself has suffered the hellish agonies of the cross. We believe that Jesus descended into hell. On the cross, Jesus suffered the full fury of divine wrath and the utter despair of being separated from his Father's love – the very essence of hell. What, in hell, has God ever done for us? He has suffered the full penalty that our sins deserve. And now, having been to hell and back for us, Jesus has the empathy of grace to give every grieving, anguished, and enraged person who has lost what they love in life.

This is at the heart of the biblical gospel. It all comes from the loving heart of God to those who are exposed and condemned by the light of his holiness. 'In this is love, not that we loved God but that he loved us.' That is where it all starts. What has this God done? He has 'sent his only Son into the world.' He has sent him into harm's way for us. He has humbled himself down to our size. He has put himself in our power. There was no room for him in the inn. He had nowhere to lay his head. He was despised and rejected of men, a man of sorrows and acquainted with grief. He was the object of envy and hatred beyond bounds. The very loveliness and purity of his life exposed the ugliness and evil that lies in the hearts of even the best of people. What did he come to do and to be?

He came to be 'the propitiation for our sins' (1 Jn. 4:10 ESV). This is the classic doctrine of penal substitution. He took our place, bore our punishment, felt the penalty that was coming our way, took the bullet and endured the outpouring of wrath that was God's righteous response to our cosmic treason. He did it to demonstrate the Father's love for us. It is this that convinces me of the love of God for me. It never fails to move me. When I am most self-absorbed, it pulls me out of myself. When I am most addicted to the things of this passing world, it draws my heart heavenwards. When I am most distant from God, it draws me back to his heart of love. And it does something else.

God's visible presence

'No-one has ever seen God' (1 Jn. 4:12). That is an absolute as well as an obvious statement. Some people saw something of God's splendour. Moses saw the afterburner of the glory of God. But some people see God because 'if we love one another, God abides in us and his love is perfected in us' (1 Jn. 4:12). Our love for one another is evidence of God's indwelling presence. 'God's love which originates in himself (7, 8) and was manifested in his Son (9, 10) is perfected in his people (12).'[49] So to the degree to which I am able, by the power of the indwelling Spirit of God, to overcome my self-seeking, self-assertion, self-sensitiveness, self-conceit, self-defence, self-sufficiency, self-pity, self-consciousness, self-righteousness, self-indulgence and self-pleasing, and am able to reach out to and serve and love my brothers and sisters in Christ, to that degree is the love of God perfected in me.

Love for others is an outworking of the gospel. It is seeing what God has done for me in spite of all my unworthiness and then my treating others with the same grace with which I have been treated myself. He loved us when we were still sinners. He did not withdraw from us but drew near to us. This transforms my attitude to difficult people. It makes me patient with those who do not grasp the Bible's teaching but still struggle with doubts, sensitive to those who struggle with sinful choices.

True unity and oneness and active love among Jesus' people are the only visible evidence God will give to people in our day of his presence in the world. And as our love for one another is active, actually reaching out to others, making sacrifices for others, serving others, so people see something of that great love with which he has loved us.

Act 3 Scene 4

In his steps

We have been using John 17 as the window into the thinking of the Father and the Son as they plan the whole movement of redemption. We have watched as the pieces in the jigsaw gradually come together, until the main character in the drama has walked on stage and gone to the cross. We have also begun to see its impact on the lives of those who are caught up in the story, those who have come to trust in Christ. It is the cross that settles their relationship with God (Romans); and it is their incentive to love one another (1 John). Now we discover that it is their support in difficult days.

Following Jesus has never been easy, although at some times and in some places it has been and is still particularly tough. When Peter wrote 'To God's elect, strangers in the world' he knew that they knew something of the cost of discipleship. 'You may have had to suffer grief in all kinds of trials,' he writes (1:6). It may come as a surprise to some Christians that God's people should ever have it rough. Turn to Christian television and you are liable to hear a kind of preaching that says, 'If you come to Jesus your problems will be resolved, and your financial worries will be solved. If you trust Jesus you will be able to buy that car you want, that house you want: you'll be healthy, wealthy and wise.' Becoming a Christian leads to a better life here. One popular book says it all in its title: *Your best life now*: that is right here, right now in this world.

Peter is more realistic. In fact he uses eight different words for suffering in this letter and he talks about their various trials fifteen times. He says we'll suffer for living godly lives; both for being good and doing good; and for simply confessing the name of Jesus. He urges us to be good witnesses while we live our lives in front of our persecutors. He does not write to teach us how we can get one over our persecutors or how we can out-argue them. His great passion is to teach us to be a good witness, a living testament, in front of those who are mocking, insulting, scorning and whipping us for Christ. And his key is to point us to the example of Jesus. So we need to answer the question some are asking: is this the key to what the cross is about? Is it simply to teach us to be patient sufferers?

New Testament letters were not written to provide us with systematic explanations of doctrine. We have to use them to answer those questions but they were written into specific pastoral situations and it is from what they write that we derive an idea of what they believed. We saw in studying John's letter that the atonement of our Lord was mentioned there in at least two contexts – in relation to my fellowship with God and my need to have my sin dealt with, and in relation to my need to love my brothers and sisters. I am to love them because God in Christ has loved me first and has demonstrated that self-denial and self-sacrifice lie at the heart of the eternal love of God.

Peter is doing something similar in his first letter. It is dense with references to the atonement of Christ, but the context of these references is in teaching about other matters of Christian living. So he refers to Christ's work of redemption when he is talking about the behaviour of servants, or the Christian's response to undeserved suffering or when he is making general assertions about Christian living. Peter is convinced that the atonement, the death of Christ, has practical force in the life of the believer. He uses at least five types of metaphor, most of which we have noted before, to explain what Christ was doing on the cross. He roots his argument on the unfolding drama of redemption. And what links these metaphors together is the idea of substitution or representation, where one party or thing stands in place of, or works on behalf of, another.[50] This is consistent with the developing theme we've been noting in our review of the Bible's teaching; it is what we would have expected. If there has been one dominant note or consistent theme to the drama so far, it is that Jesus died in the place of his people, bearing the penalty due to their sin.

Submit like the Servant

Christians are called to live differently from the world. This applies to the way we view the state: 'Submit yourselves for the Lord's sake to every authority instituted among men: whether to the king, as the supreme authority . . .' (2:13). Many of the people in the churches he was writing to were slaves and had been converted to Christianity. They were asking the question, 'How do I live as a slave, especially if my master is harsh? What do I do? Do I ignore them; disobey them; kill them?' Peter tells them to 'submit yourselves to your

masters with all respect, not only to those who are good
and considerate, but also to those who are harsh' (1 Pet.
2:18). They should avoid bad behaviour: why? 'But how
is it to your credit if you receive a beating for doing
wrong and endure it? But if you suffer for doing good
and you endure it, this is commendable before God. To
this you were called, because Christ suffered for you,
leaving you an example, that you should follow in his
steps' (2:20–22). So they are to respond with respect,
obedience and endurance. And it's in that context he
talks about Jesus who is the Servant of all; he is the ideal
Servant. They are to think like Jesus did, who was *the*
Servant par excellence.

The representative substitute

The background to this reference is the Servant of the
Lord described in Isaiah 40–55. That passage, which as
we have seen is consistent with the developing teaching
about the purpose of God in Christ, is about a
representative substitute taking the place of his people.
That is to say, Christ is both our representative and our
substitute.

> For to this you have been called, because Christ also
> suffered for you, leaving you an example, so that you might
> follow in his steps. He committed no sin, neither was deceit
> found in his mouth. When he was reviled, he did not revile
> in return; when he suffered, he did not threaten, but
> continued entrusting himself to him who judges justly. He
> himself bore our sins in his body on the tree, that we might
> die to sin and live to righteousness. By his wounds you have
> been healed. For you were straying like sheep, but have now
> returned to the Shepherd and Overseer of your souls
> (2:21–25 ESV).

Our Lord was suffering 'for you,' says Peter. Here
again the word 'for' (Greek: 'anti') has the idea of 'in
place of' or 'as a substitute for.' What was he doing? 'He
himself bore our sins in his body on the tree.' It was *our*
sins' borne 'in *his* body.' Once again he is echoing Isaiah
53 and means that Jesus went through the appropriate
punishment for our sins in place of us. 'For Christ also
suffered once for (concerning) sins, the righteous for (on
behalf of) the unrighteous, that he might (in order that he
might) bring us to God' (3:18 ESV). Bringing unrighteous
people (that is, those who deserved suffering) to God first
required the righteous bringer to suffer in their stead.[51]
Knowing that my sin has been dealt with; understanding
that there is no judgement to face; will transform my fear
of death and make me willing to face anything for him.

The leading example

'Christ suffered for you, leaving you an example that you
should follow in his steps' (2:21). He is the forerunner, the
one who goes ahead to blaze a trail for those who follow
him, the one whose footsteps we are to follow. It's the
picture of someone making his way through a minefield;
if we put our steps where he has put his we shall be safe.
The job of the believer is simply to *follow* him. Following
is what discipleship is all about.

There is an old heresy that goes back to a man called
Grotian. He developed the 'governmental' view of the
atonement. This taught that Christ suffered as an
example to show us what a terrible thing sin is. That is
not what Peter has in mind here. Christ suffered in our
place and as our representative so that we might be freed
from condemnation but also so that we might become
connected to him and conformed to his likeness. We see

this in 2:24: 'He himself bore our sins in his body on the tree, that we might die to sin and live to righteousness.' 'As Christ was an obedient servant on behalf of Christians, Christians are to be obedient servants as his followers.'[52]

Peter, who was an eyewitness, has a lot to say about what Christ had to go through as he suffered for our sin (2:23–24). Jesus had to go through hell for us. Arrested in the middle of the night, rushed into a kangaroo court; found guilty on inadequate evidence; and sent first to the king and then to the Roman governor, he was put through all kinds of injustice. He was mocked and vilified, beaten and bloodied, and all because he was acting as our substitute, our representative. He was where we should have been, taking that on the chin for us.

Most of us today are spared that kind of experience. We have laws to ensure that our employers don't whip us. The reference to 'wounds' in verse 24 had a literal relevance both to Jesus and to the many who read Peter's letter. But even with all the legislative protection in the world, there is still injustice around. Often we are put through emotional suffering, if not physical, and we can identify with Christ's suffering in reality and not just in theory. And when we are going through the mill, we are called to take his approach, to live the way he did. When we get into trouble as one of Jesus' people, how are we to respond? Peter says we're to respond the way Jesus did. They hurled their insults at him, but he did not retaliate. He suffered, but he made no threats. He entrusted himself to the one who judges justly. Peter is saying that it is never right for Christians to defend themselves with force. He had learned that the night Jesus was betrayed and the soldiers had come with an army to arrest him. When the soldiers approached to arrest Jesus, Peter who was always a little boisterous and enthusiastic, leapt out there in front of about five hundred soldiers, fully armed, ready to take them on. And Peter was told to put his sword away. 'We don't do that,' Jesus said. And later when Jesus is in front of Pilate he says, 'My kingdom is not of this world or else my servants would fight.'

So when the Pope issued a bull saying he wanted armies to go and retake Jerusalem in a crusade, he was being unChristlike. And when the parliamentary army marched to Scotland and the Presbyterian and parliamentary army of England were facing one another on the field singing the same psalm, committed to the same reformation and the same confession of faith, and then fought one another, they were acting in an unChristlike way. And when the liberation theologians of Latin America encouraged a form of Christian terrorism, they were not acting like Christ.

This also applies to our response when we are under verbal attack in the media. Paul tells us to 'Bless those who persecute you; bless and do not curse. Rejoice with those who rejoice; mourn with those who mourn. Live in harmony with one another . . . Do not repay anyone evil for evil.' Leave that to God, and 'overcome evil with good' (Rom. 12:14–16, 17, 21). There is not one hint that Christians should ever resort to violence to defend or propagate their faith: rather, like Christ himself, they should suffer in great patience, confident in God.

Jesus suffered patiently and humbly but he also 'continued entrusting himself to him who judges justly.' He looked forward to the day of vindication. We are to be like him in enduring now, with an eye to the day of judgement when all the inequities will be put right; when God will vindicate all his abused and misused people. He explains what he means 'So then, those who suffer according to God's will should commit themselves to their faithful Creator and continue to do good' (1 Pet. 4:19). The cross of Jesus gets us ready for whatever the world might throw at us.

Acceptable sacrifices

Peter draws from the temple ritual to show us how our service can be acceptable to God. He opens his letter by echoing Jesus' own words in John 17, by describing Father, Son and Spirit all conspiring together to save a people from the world. Together they work to bring about 'sprinkling with his blood' (1 Pet. 1:2). The background to this was a great covenant ceremony held by Moses. All the people of God are gathered before him. He builds an altar and offers sacrifices. Half the blood is sprinkled on the altar, and the other half is sprinkled on the people. This was an indication that the people have been cleansed and the problem between them and God has been resolved. Then Moses declares: 'Behold the blood of the covenant which the Lord has made with you' (Ex. 24:8 ESV). So we are God's people today, the people of the covenant, a covenant sealed, not with animal blood, but by Jesus' blood.

He talks about 'the precious blood of Christ, a lamb without blemish or defect' (1:19). We have seen this image before at the Passover, when only those who killed the firstborn lamb and dabbed its blood on the doorposts were spared. The New Testament makes many allusions to this event. It was a sign and a symbol. The only place that is safe is if we are hiding in Jesus, the lamb of God, who takes away the sin of the world. The redeeming death of Jesus saves, guards, and marks the people of God today. This explains how we are able to come to God (1 Pet. 2:4). Because the barrier has been removed, because our sin has been punished in him, it is therefore covered by him and we are enabled to 'offer spiritual sacrifices acceptable to God through Jesus Christ' (1 Pet. 2:5 ESV). That last phrase is the key, 'through Jesus Christ.' All our worship and prayers and service are acceptable to God because of our Saviour's accomplishment on our behalf. We can talk of serving humanity in God's name, and we should; we can talk about offering worship to God, and we should, but we should not forget that what makes such service and worship pleasing is not our offering it or doing it, but Christ through whom it is offered and in whose name it is done.

Holy blood, Holy God

The cross should make a difference to the way we live. God calls us to be holy; to be holy is to be marked out as belonging to God. It goes right to the roots of the way we think, the way we live, and the way we perceive the world. Holiness begins with a transformation on the inside and then begins to spill out on the outside. How can we be holy? We can only be holy if God owns us, and to own us he must redeem us. What does it cost to redeem us? Peter quotes what may well have been a creedal statement or a liturgical prayer. Believers were 'redeemed from the empty way of life handed down to you from your forefathers . . . with the precious blood of Christ, a lamb without blemish or defect' (1:18–19). God rescues his people through ransom and redemption. We have seen that this is language Jesus himself used, 'the Son of Man came to give himself as a ransom for many.' And Isaiah speaks of a ransom, 'For thus says the Lord: "You were sold for nothing, and you shall be ransomed without money"' (Is. 52:3 ESV).' The redemption price is spelled out in the next chapter (Is. 53) – the suffering of the Lord's Servant. So the cost of our redemption was immense.

We have been brought to God and brought out of an old way of life. We should therefore live as those who have been redeemed, remembering the price that was paid and not squandering it. He's appealing to us to be holy by appealing to two great emotions in our hearts. He's saying that Christians lead holy lives because of love, because we've understood what it cost God to possess us. And we should live a holy life out of fear because we're afraid of abusing the love of God.

The mediator

A mediator is someone involved in conflict resolution; he brings enemies together and reconciles them to one another. In 1 Peter 3:18 we have an indirect reference to this role of Christ. 'For Christ also suffered once for sins, the righteous for the unrighteous, that he might bring us to God' (ESV). Here the key idea is 'to bring us to God.' We have seen that to be our human problem; we are separated from God. The angel outside Eden carries a sword to bar the way back to paradise. The curtain hangs in the Temple to bar the way into the Holy Place, the throne room of God. Our sins cut us off from fellowship with God, they keep us distant. Above all, God's Holy nature is offended by our sin. So, Christ comes to deal with our 'sins.' His substitutionary suffering is essential to deal with the sin problem. As a result of Christ's work for us, the problem is resolved, the punishment is taken for us, and we can be reconciled to God and God to us.

Just how effective is Christ's work as mediator? People who were once 'not a people' have now become 'God's people' (1 Pet. 2:10). Former enmity has turned to friendship. Because Christ has reconciled us to God, we should approach him in worship and serve him with our lives.

This idea of reconciliation is also found in Paul and is linked to propitiation

> in Christ God was reconciling the world to himself, not counting their trespasses against them, and entrusting to us the message of reconciliation. Therefore, we are ambassadors for Christ, God making his appeal through us. We implore you on behalf of Christ, be reconciled to God. For our sake he made him to be sin who knew no sin, so that in him we might become the righteousness of God' (2 Cor. 5:19–21 ESV).

Christ the victor

Peter has been expounding the Christians' confidence. What Christ has done resolves all the outstanding issues with respect of God. Our relationship with him is now established. Because of this we can face anything and we are also ready to live differently for his glory. He has just one more metaphor to use of the death of Christ; this time as the Victor. This was one of the popular ways of thinking about Christ's death in the early centuries of Christianity. Peter mentions it here in 3:18–21, 'Christ also suffered for sins ... being put to death in the flesh but made alive in the spirit, in which he went and proclaimed to the spirits in prison ... who has gone into heaven and is at the right hand of God, with angels, authorities, and powers having been subjected to him' (ESV). Most likely this is Christ proclaiming his victory to the evil spirits held in chains of darkness. Here is the flow of the thought. In dealing with our sins, Christ is also dealing decisively with our enemies and his.

We have come under bondage to the evil one; we are not only children of wrath, we are the children of the serpent. The apostle John makes this point in his first letter. Satan's hold over our lives is our sinful nature. This is what he makes his base of operations in all his attacks upon us. Satan's power over us is broken because Christ has dealt with our sin by his death in our place.

Satan is described as the accuser of God's people. Part of his power is blackmailing the guilty. But now our sin is removed and placed on Christ, we are free from his power. His death clears us of guilt. So the accuser has nothing left to accuse us of.

As sinners he also uses the fear of death to keep us in bondage. It is fear of death that shuts our mouths and keeps us from being sold out for God. It makes us compromise in order to squeeze out a few more minutes of life. It ties us to things and people here and robs us of joy in eternity. But by his death and resurrection, Jesus has also decisively secured our resurrection, so that because he lives we shall live also. Therefore there is nothing Satan can hold over us. Satan is a defeated enemy. 'There is no liberation from the power of Satan unless there is propitiation that deals with our fear of the wrath of God, and expiation of our guilt'.[53]

If Jesus has not dealt with sin on the cross there would be no victory. In other words, it all hinges on Jesus taking my punishment, experiencing my penalty, then dealing with sin and its penalty and punishment. It's that which removes Satan's grip from my life, takes it away and gives me perfect freedom. It is knowing that Christ has triumphed over all the powers, of sin, Satan and death that assures me of my ultimate victory in him. He 'has gone into heaven and is at the right hand of God, with angels, authorities, and powers having been subjected to him' (1 Pet. 3:22 ESV).

There is no need to avoid the implication of what Christ has done. Is Christ the Servant? In acting as our Saviour and Sin-bearer he also acts as our example. He is our model of how to suffer for and serve God. He did not pay back evil for evil; he endured. That's going to be the hardest thing that we will have to do. To be a Christian is to turn the other cheek, it is the part of the servant. Is Christ the Redeemer? Because we are now God's possession it's possible for us to be radically holy people. Is Christ the Mediator? We should draw near to God through him in prayer, praise and worship. Is Christ the Victor? Then we should never fear death or what people can do to us since we will have a better resurrection.

Act 3 Scene 5

Our great high priest

We began our drama by overhearing our Lord speaking to his Father just before his arrest on the night he was betrayed. Since the time of the early church fathers, this prayer has been known as the high priestly prayer of Jesus Christ. There are a number of reasons for this. It was offered by our Lord on the occasion of his consecrating himself as both priest and victim in the approaching sacrifice of the cross. 'For their sake I consecrate myself,' he says (Jn. 17:19 ESV). As we have seen, on the Day of Atonement, Israel's high priest would pray for himself, his fellow priests and the covenant community (Lev. 16:6, 33). So our high priest prayed for himself (Jn. 17:1–5), the disciples (Jn. 17:6–19) and the whole believing community from their day till the end of history, 'those who will believe in me through their word' (Jn. 17: 20–26). The consecration of the high priest and the sacrificial victim led to the whole community of Israel being declared clean or sanctified. So Jesus prays, 'I consecrate myself that they also may be sanctified in truth.'

It seems that the dramatic ministry of the high priest in Israel was simply a dress rehearsal for the real act. Nowhere is that made clearer than in the Letter to the Hebrews. Christ's priesthood is mentioned there either explicitly or implicitly in all thirteen chapters. Many of the themes that have emerged in earlier chapters are brought into sharper focus by this writer. Following our Lord in John 17, this writer has a view of the greatness of God that colours all of his thinking. If Jesus regarded his Father as being Holy and Righteous, the book of Hebrews has been shaped by that perspective. It is true that most of the book shows us what God has done to bring human beings to salvation and demonstrates the love of God. But, as elsewhere in Scripture, that love is not taken for granted. The writer places that love in the context of a much richer and therefore truer picture of who God is.

So we find descriptions of the awfulness and holiness of God. He transcends space and time. He stands at an infinite moral distance from men and women in their sin. Hebrews sees the Old Testament revelation of God as an essential backdrop against which to understand what God has done for us in Christ. It describes the living God who is there; whose word is living and active and sharper than a two-edged sword, who cannot be simply ignored. He stands astride all that he has made as its Creator and Lord. To serve him requires the best we have: puny people must not dare to give him their cast-offs. It shows how desperate sin is and how far from him we are by nature. He contrasts the amazing privileges of the believer today with the experiences of Moses in the past

For you have not come to what may be touched, a blazing fire and darkness and gloom and a tempest and the sound of a trumpet and a voice whose words made the hearers beg that no further messages be spoken to them. For they could not endure the order that was given, 'If even a beast touches the mountain, it shall be stoned' (Heb. 12:18–20 ESV).

We find echoes of Jesus' own approach to his Father in the awe and reverence with which God is described, 'It is a fearful thing to fall into the hands of the living God,' or again, 'for our God is a consuming fire' (Heb. 10:31; 12:29 ESV). Here is a God who is apart from us in terms of being and nature; above is in terms of authority and control; and against us in terms of sin and judgement. In fact here lies our biggest problem: 'it is appointed for man to die once, and after that comes judgement' and it is God who is 'the Judge of all' (Heb. 9:27; 12:23 ESV). Just as our Lord himself was conscious that we people would have to stand one day before his Holy and Righteous Father, so the writer to Hebrews knows that God is great and God is holy and that his judgement is a searching judgement for he discerns 'the thoughts and intentions of the heart and no creature is hidden from his sight, but all are naked and exposed to the eyes of him to whom we must give an account' (Heb. 4:12–13 ESV).

This, as it has been throughout the story so far, is the proper backdrop to the revelation of the mercy and compassion of God. Hebrews is full of God's gracious and loving eagerness to see his people saved. His throne is one of grace and mercy and it is God himself who has provided us with a way of salvation in Christ, and who himself first spoke about it to human beings (Heb. 4:16; 2:3). Our salvation came about in fulfilment of his promises to Abraham, according tothe terms of the covenant he made, solemnly contracting to save men and women through the work of his own Son, for he is 'faithful who had promised' (Heb. 11:11 ESV).

It is the writer to Hebrews who describes something of the great sweep of Christ's work. God saves us through the Son who is the 'radiance of the glory of God and the exact imprint of his nature' who 'upholds the universe by the word of his power' (Heb. 1:3 ESV). This Son is Almighty God and stands before all time and all things. He is superior to the angels, the highest beings in the order of creation; and he is a prophet over Moses, the greatest prophet of them all. In particular, it is as a priest that he stands over and above the now obsolete Levitical priesthood. But the Lord became a human being in order that he might die for his people, 'the children' the Father had given him. Jesus came to be both priest and victim; offerer and offering. 'Therefore he had to be made like his brothers in every respect, so that he might become a merciful and faithful high priest in the service of God' (Heb. 2:17). He was 'for a little while made lower than the angels' so that 'by the grace of God he might taste death for everyone' (Heb. 2:7–9 ESV).

In his humanity, the sinless Lord Jesus suffered at every point of his earthly life. Every day he felt the perturbations caused by living in a sinful world; he knew disappointments and sorrows, physical pains and frustrations of spirit; he grew weary and sore and must often have longed for home and comforts; he was lied to, falsely reproved, argued with, disliked and cheated. The earthly temptations which he endured in the wilderness and at other times (Lk.4:13) from the devil, and daily from the 'opposition from sinful men' (12:3), including even his own disciples, made him a sympathetic priest. But it was especially during the last few hours that he was exposed to the extreme of physical and spiritual torture. Hebrews 5:7 describes the 'loud cries and tears' that Jesus offered in the garden of Gethsemane. The divine Son had to become fully human in order to suffer and die as a human. And why did he die? In order that 'through death he might destroy the one who has the power of death, that is the devil, and deliver all those who through fear of death were subject to lifelong slavery.' And he did this by making 'propitiation for the sins of the people' (2:14–17 ESV). Christ, by taking first humanity then sin upon himself, has averted God's wrath from his people. Like the rest of Scripture, as we have seen, Hebrews sees the ideas of substitution and satisfaction as being the controlling themes of the atonement. But whereas Paul writes to the Romans using the forensic language of the courtroom familiar to any citizen of Rome, the writer to Hebrews prefers to use the cultic language of the temple more familiar to Jews.

Between Heaven and Earth

Hebrews encourages us to think primarily about the work of our great high priest; in fact this is '*the* main point' of his letter (Heb. 8:1). Our high priest is great because of who he is: that is, his essential nature as the God-Man, God with skin on. He is also great because of what he has accomplished. 'He makes propitiation for sins of the people.' And he has passed through the created heavens 'into heaven itself, now to appear in the presence of God on our behalf' (9:24 ESV). God has enthroned him in the place of supreme power and authority, therefore he is well able to meet all our needs; and, because he is there for us his presence makes it possible for us to approach God in prayer now and live in his presence for eternity. For the Christian this means that we can come boldly and with 'confidence' to the 'throne of grace' and find mercy for our sinfulness and help for our weakness (4:14–16).

Our unique high priest is qualified to help us by virtue of his being both God and man. Both his deity and humanity are genuine. In his humanity, he shares a fellow feeling with us; he understands our limitations; he has a capacity to 'feel' with us in our day-to-day struggles. He too learned the full meaning of obedience in practice in his life and the demands and discipline involved in fully human experience. On the other hand, he supersedes all other priests because he is God the Son, and unlike them, he has no personal sin to distance him from a holy God. They had to offer sacrifices for their own sins first before sacrificing on behalf of others.

The Lord Jesus occupies a higher priesthood than the Old Testament one. In the central chapters of Hebrews we are introduced to the enigmatic figure of Melchizedek, who is presented as a type of Christ. He appears out of the blue, without mention of genealogy, birth or death. So he stands on the pages of Scripture as an eternal figure who points us to Jesus. Jesus is God the Son, the sinless man and the Lord's anointed Servant, directly and personally chosen by God. He acts as a priest eternally; for 'there will never dawn a day when he will cease to be alive, available and active.'[54] Jesus' priesthood is eternal since he lives 'in the power of an endless life'. Melchizedek was also a king; in fact his name means 'king of righteousness' and he is also 'king of Salem' or 'peace.' Because our Lord Jesus does his work in righteousness he is able to bless us with peace. So Jesus is more than qualified to be our great high priest and in every way he is able to offer a sacrifice far greater and more effective than all the sacrifices of the Old Testament period.

The one sacrifice for sins

Whereas Paul in Romans focused on sin in terms of transgression and condemnation, the focus of Hebrews is on the complementary ideas of sin as defilement and banishment; this arises out of his focus on the Holy Place where God dwells. Perhaps he has in mind the Psalm 24 with its question and answer: 'Who shall ascend the hill of the Lord? And who shall stand in his Holy Place? He who has clean hands and a pure heart!' But what if your heart is not pure, what can be done? The answer is in the sacrifice Christ offers for us.

Illustrations have their limits. A visit to an earthly monarch requires that you get cleaned up on the outside: to draw near to the King of Heaven necessitates a clean-up on the inside. The former has to do with show; the latter has to do with holiness. Illustrations can be very useful, especially if they are illustrations (unlike mine) that God himself has given us. In Hebrews 8–10, the writer explains how the Old Testament system of priests and sacrifices was an important illustration, given by God to teach how difficult it is for people like us to draw near to God. By his very nature, he defines all that is good, moral, and right, and he is a God of absolute holiness. On the other hand, the Old Testament system of priests and sacrifices illustrated that we are fundamentally defiled and distanced from him. Doing what comes naturally to us leaves us mud-covered and dirt-splattered on the inside. It leaves us banished from his sight, since he is of purer eyes than to behold iniquity; so the whole ritual of the temple was to keep sinners out of the Holy Place. The fact of sacrifice demonstrated over and over again that the wages of sin is death. But it also demonstrated how ineffective that system was; after all, it had to be repeated year after year, for centuries.

Just consider the inadequacies of the old system for a moment. To begin with, the earthly temple was never God's permanent address. 'The Most High does not dwell in houses made by hands' (Acts 7:48 ESV). It never gave ordinary worshippers access, except to the outer court where they were left feeling like outsiders. Only the high priest, once a year on the Day of Atonement (as we have seen) was able to enter and only if he took blood with him. All this goes to show that the way into the real sanctuary was not open and that full fellowship with God was impossible (Heb. 9:7–9). And it also showed that the sacrifices didn't reach the parts that really mattered. All they achieved was a ceremonial cleansing 'of the flesh' not a moral cleansing of the innermost being. And what is worse, 'it is impossible for the blood of bulls and goats to take away sins' (Heb.10:2–4). There was this planned deficiency right at the heart of that Old Testament operation. Why? Because it only ever was meant to be a pointer to the real thing, part of the teaching programme to help us understand what Christ was doing when he came and died. It was only the 'copy' of the real thing.

So what did Christ do? He 'entered heaven itself,' that is, the place where God, in all his fullness, lives in all his glory; where holiness reigns and we are excluded. Jesus has entered the Holy Place 'through' his blood, that is, in virtue of his death or of his sacrifice already offered; and he has entered not in order to secure redemption, but as one who has already secured it.[55]

When Jesus was explaining to his disciples the meaning of his death on the night of his crucifixion, he took them back to Exodus 24, 'this is the blood of the covenant.' We know from Luke and from Paul that he also took them back to Jeremiah 31, 'this is the new covenant in my blood.' Jesus takes the disciples right where the author of Hebrews takes them to explain his death. Jesus was saying, 'If you want to understand my death, you need to understand it is the thing that brings about the promises which God prophesied hundreds of years of ago through Jeremiah and Isaiah and Ezekiel and even all the way back to Moses. I am the mediator of the new covenant.'

There is no doubt that the Old Testament sacrificial system was a gory affair. During the thousand plus years of the Old Covenant, there were more than a million animals slaughtered. So considering each bull's gallon or two of blood, and each goat's quart, the Old Covenant rested on a sea of blood. During the Passover period a trough was erected from the temple down into the Kedron Valley for the disposal of blood – a kind of sacrificial plumbing system.

Why so much blood? Because the governing principle in relation to transgressions is, 'without the shedding of blood there is no forgiveness of sins' (9:22 ESV). The blood proclaims that God takes sin seriously; it is a capital offence. In the blood ritual of the Bible, blood is not a means of sharing in life (like a blood transfusion), but it is evidence of life taken or sacrificed in violent death. It is evidence of the penalty of sin duly exacted and fully paid. What procures the remission of sin is the actual blood-shedding; and what redeems us from our transgressions is the death which has occurred. Every time we celebrate Communion and hear these words 'This cup is the new covenant in my blood which is poured out for you for the forgiveness of sins . . . drink of it, all of you' we are hearing Jesus' explanation of why he had to die. He is saying that we are in covenant with God, we violated that covenant, we deserve to die, and that he came to die in our place.

Every time we come to that table, we remember that we are in fellowship with the Father, not because of anything that we have done, but because of what Christ has done. He died the death of a covenant-breaker, even though he remained perfectly faithful to it, so that all covenant-breakers who believe on him alone for salvation might be brought into fellowship with God. There is therefore no need to repeat the sacrifice. He 'entered once for all into the Holy Place;' 'he has appeared once for all at the end of the ages to put away sins by the sacrifice of himself.' There is now for those who believe total forgiveness, and 'where there is forgiveness of these there is no longer any offering for sin' (Heb. 9:12, 26; 10:18 ESV).

He sat down . . .

Jesus has gained decisive and permanent entrance into the very presence of God. Because he is the sinless man as well as a lamb without blemish, his blood can purify our consciences from defilement and give us freedom to serve the living God. The one sacrifice of Christ, once offered, has sufficient virtue to cover and cleanse, to 'put away' all the sins of God's people till the end of time. His death has secured an eternal redemption for us (Heb. 9:26 ESV).

Everything about Jesus' work speaks reality. He went into the actual presence of God and there he stays for the entire universe to see that he is perfectly acceptable in God's sight. There he is exalted. The writer to Hebrews is setting us up for the final revelation of Jesus given us in the Bible. Right now he appears 'in the presence of God on our behalf' (Heb. 9:24 ESV). He never forgets us, he continues to support us. He feels for us still; he understands the things that make it difficult for us to resist temptation. He prays for us now, because he knows what human life is like and how much we must often bear. As our advocate with the Father, he is our ever present friend and companion.

He will appear a second time not to 'bear sin but to bring salvation' and this is where we are now. We are like the first disciples standing looking up towards heaven, waiting expectantly for the Lord to return and take the power and reign.

Act 3 Scene 6

The lamb wins

John 17 begins and ends with glory. Jesus speaks to his Father about 'the glory I had with you before the world existed' (Jn. 17:5 ESV). It ends with Jesus asking, 'Father, I desire that that they also, whom you have given me, may be with me where I am, to see my glory that you have given me because you loved me before the foundation of the world' (Jn. 17:24 ESV). At the beginning of the scene there is only the Father and the Son and the Spirit, enjoying a perfect relationship, but at the end of the chapter others have joined them on stage: those who come to believe in the Son. They see and share his glory.

It's a great picture. The whole sweep of history is there, encapsulated in that one chapter. It gives us an insight into the mind of God. Here the Father and the Son are talking together about this great plan of redemption, a plan formed in eternity and executed in time in the person of the Lord Jesus, to be consummated when it reached its fulfilment 'in a new heavens and earth.'

Peter saw the work of Christ for us as an incentive to persevere in days of real trial and Hebrews saw Jesus

entering heaven for us and exalted to the very presence
and throne of God by virtue of his work on the cross.
Both are looking at Christ's work from our standpoint,
and we are left looking up towards heaven for our
coming inheritance.

In Revelation however John is given a 'heaven's eye'
view of the unfolding plan of redemption. We are usually
daunted by this book and long for a key to unlock its
secrets. We are right to be, for the simple reason that it
takes us boldly where no human being has gone before,
into the throne room of the universe. It lets us see things
that are beyond our finite minds to comprehend, so the
revelation is given in signs and symbols. We have seen
God use various forms of speech to communicate with us
in the course of our journey – narration, poetry and
letters; but Revelation introduces us to another form.
Apocalyptic literature is full of pictures, signs and
symbols. It is a 'revelation of Jesus Christ,' given by God
'to show to his servants the things that must soon take
place' (Rev. 1:1 ESV). We are not meant to visualise the
pictures we see in Revelation but to interpret them in
light of Scripture.

Its theme is the triumph of God in Christ. In this book
the word for victory always stands alone, and absolutely.
Jesus is the Victor in a far more complete and final sense
than was ever true of any emperor or general. And
throughout this book we are never allowed to forget for a
moment the absolute sovereignty of God.

Revelation does what is written on the packet: it
reveals Jesus Christ and is rich with titles which describe
his person and work. Our Lord is 'the faithful witness,
the firstborn of the dead, and the ruler of the kings on
earth.' He is 'the Son of man,' 'the first and the last,' 'the
living one' who 'holds the keys of Death and Hades.' He
is the one who 'holds the seven stars in his right hand,'

'the first and the last who died and came to life,' 'who has
the seven spirits of God,' 'the holy one, the true one, who
has the key of David,' the 'faithful and true witness, the
beginning of God's creation.' All those come from the
opening three chapters. In chapter 19 alone he is called
'Faithful and True,' 'the Word of God,' 'King of kings and
Lord of lords.' It seems that no one title can capture the
sheer worth of our Lord Jesus. Nothing is sufficient in our
language, in any language, to say what is so spectacular
about Jesus. He exceeds all our categories of thought, yet
God has been pleased to reveal to us something of the
glory of his person through these titles and descriptors he
is given.

The lion king

In Revelation 4 and 5, John is given a vision of heaven
itself; in it he sees a montage of images and strange
creatures. The images he sees come straight out of the
Hebrew Scriptures. Here we have Ezekiel's 'living
beings' and Isaiah's 'elders' surrounding the heavenly
throne of God. God is sitting on the throne and in his
hand he has a book.[56] The issue is this: who is worthy to
open the book? This is either the 'book of life' in which
are recorded all the names of God's redeemed people,[57] or
it is the book that contains the plan of redemption and
judgement.[58] Whatever the precise interpretation, there is
no doubt that the book has cosmic significance. It has to
do with God's redeemed people and the unfolding will of
God in bringing about their salvation, including
judgements on the world. Who in all creation has the
authority to take the book out of God's hand? Who may
open it and begin to execute God's plan for the
redemption of his people and the judgement of the

world? Who's going to do it? Who has the authority? The situation is summed up: 'No one in heaven or on earth or under the earth was able to open the scroll or to look into it' (Rev. 5:3 ESV). No one was worthy.

It breaks John's heart and he begins to weep. It seems as if God's purposes must be thwarted. Perhaps for John the grief was even greater as he must have wondered why his Saviour was not there to save the day. At first glance, it must have seemed to him that history would not be governed in the interest of the church and that there would be 'no protection for God's children in the hours of bitter trial; no judgements upon a persecuting world; no ultimate triumph for believers; no new heaven and earth; no future inheritance!'[59] No wonder he tells us: 'I began to weep loudly because no one was found worthy to open the scroll or to look into it' (Rev. 5:4 ESV). It seemed as if God's plans were never going to be implemented; God's unfolding plan of redemption for the world was never going to be effective in history.

Then a heavenly voice responds to the apostle's tears: 'And one of the elders said to me, Weep no more; behold, the Lion of the tribe of Judah, the Root of David, has conquered, so that he can open the scroll and its seven seals' (Rev. 5:5). These titles describe God's Messiah-King who has 'conquered' or 'overcome' his enemies. This puts Christ/Messiah in a sovereign position to put into action God's plan of redemption and judgement. John is excited. He knows that his Lord Jesus is the Lion of Judah and the Son of David; he had heard even the demon-possessed people cry out 'Son of David'. He's heard blind people cry out 'Son of David.' He turns to see the king and what does he see?

A lamb standing as though it had been slain . . .

John expects to see the lion but instead sees 'a lamb standing, as though it had (just) been slain' (v 6 ESV). He is approaching the throne of God, fresh from his slaughter, having been raised from the dead. Some scholars think that here we have a heaven's eye view of Jesus' ascension into heaven. The lamb of God has come from the fight to take his power and reign. We have to grasp the juxtaposition of these two images of lion and lamb. It must have jarred on John to have these images clash in this way, the lion's strength and the lamb slaughtered, bleeding, slain.

Of all the titles of Christ in the Book of Revelation, none is as prominent as that of the lamb (it appears 28 times in this book). It has clear Old Testament precedents. There is the lamb Abraham promised to his son Isaac when he was taking him to the place of sacrifice: 'God will provide a lamb, my son,' he said. God did intervene but it wasn't a lamb. The lamb was still to be provided. Then there was the Passover lamb, slain instead of the firstborn that secured the liberty of God's people. And there is the reference in Isaiah 53: 'led like a lamb to the slaughter, and as a sheep before her shearers is silent . . .' The word used for lamb here is linked to the Aramaic word for servant, which fits the Isaiah context of the servant-lamb. And in Jeremiah 11:19 there are words that are also likely a link with this: 'I had been like a gentle lamb led to the slaughter.' Justin Martyr links these two texts in the early second century.[60] With these links established, it's not surprising to find that the Book of Revelation brings many of the strands of truth we have noted so far together and leads us to the dramatic conclusion of the story.

The lamb liberates from bondage

John opens his book with a doxology a hymn of praise to Christ, 'To him who loves us and has freed us from our sins by his blood and made us a kingdom, priests to (serve) his God and Father' (1:5–6). What is the link with chapter 5? John wrote his introduction to his book after he had received the visions, after he had seen the lamb upon his throne. This is his reflection on the vision he had received. He puts the emphasis on the Son's love: 'to him who loved us,' he writes. This is nothing new. Paul tells us that Christ 'loved the church and gave himself up for her.' It is love for us that led the Saviour to 'lay down his life for the sheep' (Jn 10:15). 'He has freed us from our sins by his blood.' Whenever we see the word 'blood' it always refers to violent death as a sacrifice; to life violently taken in our place, as he dies our death. Why does he do that? He loves us and he sheds his blood for us to liberate us from our bondage (Rev. 1:5, 6). Jesus said that 'everyone who sins is a slave to sin' (Jn. 8: 34–36) while Paul speaks of being 'enslaved to sin' (Rom. 6:16–23). Our liberation comes through Christ.

Revelation also sees sin as a 'debt' owed to God. We have already noted that this idea came straight from Jesus himself. In Matthew 6:12 he taught us to pray 'Forgive us our debts, as we forgive our debtors.' As another scholar has written

> Sin may be conceived as a charge taken out against God's holiness or justice, each of our misdeeds placing us further and further in God's debt. The debt must be repaid or the 'borrower' will be 'paid back' with judgement. The idea is close to propitiation in that it conceives of God, or his justice, as the offended party who must be compensated.[61]

Here the language is not taken from the temple or the sacrificial system but from the financial markets. Later on in chapter 18, Babylon's 'sins are heaped high as heaven, and God has remembered her iniquities.' The judgement on her is this: 'Pay her back as she herself has paid back others, and repay her double for her deeds; mix a double portion for her in the cup she mixed' (Rev. 18:5, 6 ESV). Elsewhere the idea of payback time is found in Jesus' words to the churches: 'I will repay each of you according to your deeds' (Rev. 2:23; 22:12). Sin's bondage is that we are in debt and cannot repay. 'Whoever sins is a slave to sin,' said Jesus. Jesus alone can, by the price of his blood, render to God perfect payment which liberates us from our indebtedness and our bondage to sin and death. Jesus liberates from bondage by paying our debt. And in setting us free, he elevates us to a new status as 'a kingdom, priests to his God and Father.'

The lamb triumphs through suffering

The appearance of the lamb as the conquering King teaches us that 'weak is the new strong' in the kingdom of God. The lion is a good symbol of power and strength but John declines to use it that way. It is in fact the lamb who overcomes and conquers.

The slain lamb represents the image of a conqueror that was mortally wounded while defeating the enemy. Notice the juxtaposition of the 'slain' lamb and his 'horns' of strength. In apocalyptic literature in general, and in this book in particular, a horned lamb is the symbol of a conqueror. To refer to Christ as a lamb, then, is for John a way of drawing attention to his triumph. The slaughtered lamb is standing before God, resurrected. He has died and has now conquered death by being resurrected from the dead. He now 'stands' before the throne of God above, but he stands as the 'slaughtered lamb' – that is his abiding condition as a result of the past act of being slain.[62] The resurrection was a victory but so was the defeat of death: it is that defeat of death by dying that gives him authority. It is his being slain together with the redemption of his people and his making them 'a kingdom and priests' which is the basis for his worthiness. The attendants in the heavenly court cannot wait to fall down before him and sing a new song of praise

> Worthy are you to take the scroll
> and to open its seals,
> for you were slain, and by your blood you ransomed people for God
> from every tribe and language and people and nation,
> and you have made them a kingdom and priests to our God,
> and they shall reign on the earth (Rev. 5:9–10 esv).

The words 'Worthy are you' were used to celebrate the Emperor's arrival. The idea of a new song echoes Psalm 98:1, 'Sing to the LORD a new song, for he has done marvellous things'. Every new act of mercy calls forth a new song of praise and gratitude.[63] This hymn, like most of the hymns in Revelation, is an interpretative summary of the meaning of the vision John sees; and at their heart is a celebration of Christ's death for his people. He bears the marks of the crucifixion in glory; that's why we preach Christ crucified. It was as the lamb of God that Jesus began to fulfil the Old Testament prophecies of the Messiah. The final victory of God in the human story began to be achieved by the suffering of the cross. Thus the apostle Paul can summarise the Christian message as 'we preach Christ crucified'.

The path of Jesus was suffering, then glory. He is both the victim and the victor. If we were to see the Lord Jesus Christ right now as he is, we would see that he bears the marks of crucifixion, even in his resurrected body. The slaughtered lamb stands in the centre of the throne of God, and he is worthy. This was of particular relevance to the people to whom John was writing. Many were being persecuted for their faith. They needed to be reassured that their destiny was his, if they persevered. Weakness is the new strength in Jesus' upside-down kingdom. Jesus' followers 'overcome' by becoming like the lamb of God himself, as they share in his suffering. This is how they are going to conquer the world – not by bullets or swords but by their willingness to suffer for Jesus.

The lamb redeems his people

The lamb is both the mighty Conqueror and the lowly victim. 'You were slain, and by your blood you ransomed people for God from every tribe and language and people and nation' (5:9). Here is a flashback to the Exodus and the blood of the Passover lamb. It was the sacrifice of the lamb and the splashing of its blood on the doorposts that turned God's judgement away from the households of the Israelites. The sacrifice was substitutionary and it averted wrath. Here the use of 'ransom' links Revelation with Jesus saying in Mark about his being the 'ransom for many' (Mk. 10:45 ESV). 'Sin incurs a debt against God's holiness and justice, which has resulted in our being sold into slavery or captivity.'[64]

By dying in our place and for us, he has made us God's possession. We belong to him. His mark is on our forehead and sets us apart from those who worship the beast (Rev. 14:1, 13:8). We are set free to be God's possessions. It is for him we live and serve. And Christ's redeemed people are taken from every part of this world. There is no racial or cultural superiority in his kingdom.

The lamb cleanses from defilement

John sees millions upon millions of people 'standing before the throne and in front of the lamb' (Rev. 7:9 ESV).We hear the collective voice of this vast multitude, crying out, 'Salvation belongs to our God, who sits on the throne and to the lamb' (Rev. 7:10 ESV). Who are these people? These are the ones 'coming out of the great tribulation' (Rev. 7:14 ESV). Where are they now? They are 'before the throne of God and serve him day and night in his temple' (Rev. 7:15 ESV).This is amazing; after centuries of being barred from the earthly temple which was only as copy of the true one, here these people are in heaven itself, in the real temple, and sheltered 'with his presence.' What has opened the way for them to be there in the presence of God? 'They have washed their robes and made them white in the blood of the lamb' (Rev. 7:14 ESV).

We know why they need to have their robes cleaned. It isn't just that they have broken God's law; it's as if we turned up at Buckingham Palace after a day in the garden, to have cucumber sandwiches and tea with her Majesty. And the guard says, 'There's no way you're coming in here; there's a dress code. Go and clean yourself up and then you can have tea.' As we have seen, sin dirties us; it defiles us. And those who have come to the Lord Jesus have been 'washed.' We're no longer defiled and dirty. Here we see the lamb dealing with sin, not as debt or bondage, but as defilement that makes us impure and therefore unfit for the presence of a holy God. The lamb washes us in his blood, which is just another way of saying that the death of Jesus for us deals with the sin issue and makes us fit for the presence of God.

And that is precisely where these believers are in John's vision. They are in the throne room of God, right in the Holy of Holies. 'Never again will they hunger, never again will they thirst . . . The lamb at the centre of the throne will be their shepherd: he will lead them to springs of living water. And God will wipe away every tear from their eyes.' The lamb of God cleanses us from defilement so that we can actually live in the presence of God. At the beginning of our story we saw human beings being banished from Eden and an angel standing guard threatening death to anyone who tried to come near. In the middle of our story we saw people kept out of the temple as a sign that sin separates people from God. But now, through Christ, people are in the Holy of Holies, they are living in the garden of God with 'springs of living water,' the sign of eternal satisfaction and fulfilment bubbling all around them and they are nearer to God than even Adam and Eve enjoyed; paradise has been restored.

The lamb judges the world

As we have watched the drama unfold we have been confronted again with the mystery of God's wrath and judgement in response to human sin. Here the mystery suddenly gets deeper.

> Then the kings of the earth and the great ones and the generals and the rich and the powerful, and everyone, slave and free, hid themselves in the caves and among the

rocks of the mountains, calling to the mountains and rocks, Fall
on us and hide us from the face of him who is seated on the
throne, and from the wrath of the lamb, for the great day of
their wrath has come, and who can stand? (Rev. 6:15–17 ESV).

This lamb is no pushover; it talks about his wrath. But
this is not surprising: there was complete unanimity
between the Father and the Son in the planning and
execution of the work of redemption. In our Lord's
earthly ministry, the Father was at work through the Son:
'I and the Father are one,' he said. 'My Father works and
I continue to work.' So also in the work of judging sin,
both the Father and the Son are engaged together. We
cannot drive a wedge between them. We cannot say that
Jesus is all love and no wrath. This passage directly
contradicts that illusion. It is one of the unique insights of
the New Testament that it is none other than Jesus the
Lamb of God who will judge the world. As Jesus himself
said, 'The Father judges no one, but has given all
judgement to the Son, that all may honour the Son as they
honour the Father' (Jn. 5:22 ESV).

Here is the lamb putting the finishing touches to God's
plan for the world. As well as saving his people, his is the
responsibility to oversee the final Day of Judgement. It is
frightening as we see the kings of the earth, the leaders,
the princes and the generals, the rich, the mighty and
'every slave and every free man'. They are 'hiding in
caves and among the rocks of the mountains.' And they
call on the mountains and the rocks, 'Fall on us and hide
us from the face of him who sits on the throne and from
the wrath of the lamb!' It is salutary to note that this is
Jesus we're talking about. There's coming a day when the
wrath of the lamb will finally consume the wicked.

The lamb overcomes the accuser

For the drama to reach its conclusion some loose ends have to be tied up. One of the crucial ones is the figure whose malign presence has haunted our story since its beginning. He had been there in the garden, speaking to Adam and Eve disguised as a serpent. He is humanity's great enemy, the devil or Satan. In Revelation 12 the curtain is pulled back on a new scene. A woman representing God's people in both Old Testament and New Testament eras gives birth to a child 'who will rule the nations with an iron sceptre' (Rev. 12:5 ESV). This child is then 'snatched up to God and his throne' (Rev. 12:4). A great war erupts in heaven, resulting in the defeat of the dragon and his subjects. 'And the great dragon was thrown down, that ancient serpent, who is called the devil and Satan, the deceiver of the whole world – he was thrown down to the earth, and his angels were thrown down with him' (12:9 ESV). They are cast out of heaven, and the defeat of the dragon is directly related to the ascension of the male child to heaven.

> And I heard a loud voice in heaven, saying, Now the salvation and the power and the kingdom of our God and the authority of his Christ have come, for the accuser of our brothers has been thrown down, who accuses them day and night before our God. And they have conquered him by the blood of the lamb and by the word of their testimony, for they loved not their lives even unto death (Rev. 12:10–11 ESV).

We can hear an echo of Jesus' words as he predicted his death and resurrection: 'Now is the time for judgement on this world; now the prince of this world will be driven out' (Jn. 12:31). The particular area of victory over Satan is hinted at in Revelation 12:9. He is quintessentially the 'accuser' of the people of God. His names 'Devil' and 'Satan' suggest that but it is also spelt out in the text. Accusations have to do with guilt. We are therefore dealing with sin as legal transgression. It is this accuser who would bring his charges against God's elect. He constantly reminds God and us of the condemnation earned by sin. By pointing constantly to our failures and sins he wants to have us cut off from God's presence forever. He is a murderer, and he gets no more pleasure than to see a soul ensnared by hell. But what has Christ done by his death? He has resolved those issues and brought us justification. 'Who can bring any charge against God's elect? It is God who justifies. Who is the one to condemn? Christ Jesus is the one who has died – more than that, who is raised – who is at the right hand of the God, who indeed is interceding for us' (Rom. 8:33, 34 ESV). We see how the Scriptures hold together wonderfully as all the threads of the story are now being drawn together.

The lamb secures our salvation

> All who dwell on earth will worship it (the 'beast' that represents antichrist), everyone whose name has not been written before the foundation of the world in the book of life of the lamb that was slain (13:8 ESV).

John describes a beast that has been given authority on earth to compel worship and to conquer the saints (Rev. 13:1, 7). Underneath the surface of all humanity there is a fundamental allergy to Jesus Christ. Read John 17 and you'll see that. Jesus himself says that 'The world hates you because it hated me first.' It can live with any other kind of religion except that of Jesus Christ. One day that rebellion will find a focus, and everyone will worship the beast; everyone will go along with the crowd. In the end it is the 'saints' that overcome. How do they do it? In the act of giving up their lives for their confession of Christ! Like their Master, they may appear weak, defeated and helpless in the eyes of the world. But through their faithfulness to death they inherit a crown of life (Rev. 2:10).

On the day of judgement it is those who would not buy into the beast's lies and worship the world's agenda whose names will be found in the Lamb's book of life. Jesus prayed in John 17 for those whom the Father had 'given' to him. He had written their names in the lamb's book of life from before the world began.

It was his eternal purpose and plan that the lamb should be slain for the people whose names are recorded in the Book of Life. Jesus is the Lamb who was slain before the foundation of the world, and Jesus' people are those whose names are written in the book before the foundation of the world. It was his eternal plan and purpose to deal with the dreadful effects of sin. Sin is portrayed in various ways in the Book of Revelation; as bondage, incalculable debt, moral defilement and legal guilt. But every one of those problems is dealt with by the work of the lamb.

Revelation resounds with the victory of the lamb. And what makes his victory so effective? It is his work on the cross. He has dealt decisively with sin – sin which alienates us from God and God from us; sin that brings death and suffering into human experience; sin that gives the devil a foothold in our lives; sin that sends men and women to hell, sin that leaves us all with a debt to God which we can never repay. How does he deal with sin? He takes our place and suffers instead of us; he pays the debt we owe to God's holiness and justice; he endures the penalty for our sin; he cleanses away the offensiveness that bars us from God's company; and he proclaims to the rulers and authorities that the debt we owed has been cancelled:

> God made (us) alive together with him, having forgiven us all our trespasses, by cancelling the record of debt that stood against us with its legal demands. This he set aside; nailing it to the cross. He disarmed the rulers and authorities and put them to open shame, by triumphing over them in him (Col. 2:13–15 ESV).

It is one of the great themes of the Bible that Christ decisively destroyed the works of the devil, by taking our sins on himself and taking our punishment, so that his power was well and truly defeated. His death was the death of death! What counts is to have our names written in God's book; 'if anyone's name was not found written in the book of life, he was thrown into the lake of fire' (Rev. 20:15 ESV).

The lamb throws a party

'Blessed are those who are invited to the marriage supper of the lamb' (Rev. 19:9 ESV). Jesus often used the party image to describe what is coming for his people. He talked about the day when he would sit down and eat and drink with us in the kingdom of God. The best parties are often linked to weddings, and the greatest wedding party of all is still to come. God's sovereign initiative brings about the marriage relationship; he 'calls' people to himself through the gospel. The bride is his church, his people. Salvation is both individual and corporate. We may be saved one by one but we are joined to the community of the redeemed. There is but one bride for Christ, the church which he redeemed by his blood. We are invited to his party. And the party is the prelude to a new dimension of living that exceeds our wildest dreams. So Revelation ends with a new heaven and a new earth, renewed and cleansed. 'And I heard a loud voice from the throne saying, "Now the dwelling of God is with men, and he [the lamb] will live with them",' and John goes on to tell us what he saw: 'I did not see a temple in the city, because the Lord God Almighty and the lamb are its temple. The city does not need the sun or the moon to shine on it, for the glory of God gives it light, and the lamb is its lamp.' 'No longer will there be any curse. The throne of God and of the lamb will be in the city, and his servants will serve him' (Rev. 21). It's our destiny, if we are children of God, to see what John saw, to see the reality of what is behind this picture language, as the church of Jesus Christ, like a bride receiving her husband, sees the one who loves them and gave himself for them.

What was it that Jesus prayed? 'Father, I pray that those that you have given me are with me where I am, and see my glory.' Now it has arrived, and Jesus' prayer on the eve of his passion has been heard and answered, and every one of his people are in on the act.

Notes

[1] R. J. Campbell, *The New Theology* (London: Chapman & Hall, 1907) pp115–116.

[2] Steve Chalke and Alan Mann, *The Lost Message of Jesus* (Grand Rapids: Zondervan, 2003).

[3] John Calvin, John's Gospel, Comment on John 17:23, *Calvin's Commentaries* (Grand Rapids, Baker Book House, 1979) Volume XVIII, p186.

[4] Robert Reymond, *A New Systematic Theology of the Christian Faith*, (STL, 1920) p463.

[5] Robert Reymond *A New Systematic Theology of the Christian Faith*, (STL, 1920) p343.

[6] Bertrand Russell, *The Autobiography of Bertrand Russell: 1914–1944* (London, 1968) pp158–159 (Italics mine).

[7] Derek Kidner, *Genesis* (Leicester: IVP, 1981) p14.

[8] D A Carson, *The Gagging of God* (Grand Rapids: Zondervan, 2002) p201.

[9] Augustine of Hippo, *The City of God*, Book XIV Chapter 28 (in *Internet Medieval Source Book*).

[10] J. A. Motyer, *Old Testament Covenant Theology* (Unpublished Paper, Theological Students Fellowship, 1973), p11.

[11] Alec Motyer, *Exodus* (Leicester: IVP, 2005), p116.

[12] Motyer, *ibid*, p116.

[13] Philip Graham Ryken, *Exodus* (Crossway Books, Wheaton, 2005) p330.

[14] Alec Motyer, *Old Testament Covenant Theology*, Unpublished lectures, p20.

[15] Alec Motyer, *Old Testament Covenant Theology* (Unpublished lectures, Theological students fellowship, 1972/73) p17.

[16] Leviticus 16:21 – NIV translates it as wickedness and the ESV translates it as iniquities.

[17] Derek Tidball, *The Message of the Cross* (Leicester: IVP, 2001) 74.

[18] Joachim Jeremais, *Eucharistic words of Jesus* (Minneapolis: Fortress press, 1977) p228.

[19] John Stott, *The Cross of Christ* (Leicester: IVP, 1986) p146.

[20] John Oswalt, *The book of Isaiah* (Grand Rapids: Wm Eerdmans, 1998) p387.

[21] Leon Morris, *The Apostolic Preaching of the Cross* (Grand Rapids: Wm. B. Eerdmans Pub. Co., 1955) p34.

[22] Margin of the Luther Bible, on 3:23ff.

[23] Leon Morris, *The Epistle to the Romans* (Grand Rapids: Wm B Eerdmans, 1988) p173.

[24] David Wells, *Above all earthly powers: Christ in a postmodern world* (Grand Rapids: Wm B Eerdmans, 2005) p225.

[25] J. I. Packer, *Knowing God* (London: Hodder & Stoughton, 1975) p170.

[26] John Stott, *The Message of Romans* (Leicester: IVP, 2001) p108.

[27] Leon Morris, *The Apostolic Preaching of the Cross* (Grand Rapids: Wm. B. Eerdmans Pub. Co., 1955) pp40–45.

[28] John Stott, *The Cross of Christ* (Leicester: Inter-Varsity Press, 1986) p108.

[29] David Wells, *Above all Earthly Powers: Christ in a postmodern world* (Grand Rapids: Wm B Eerdmans, 2005) p226.

[30] David Wells, *ibid*, p227.

[31] M. Lloyd-Jones, *Romans 3:20–4:25* (Edinburgh: Banner of Truth, 1970) p103.

[32] M. Lloyd-Jones, *Romans 3:20–4:25* (Edinburgh: Banner of Truth, 1970) p76.

[33] Cranfield, quoted in John Stott, *The Message of Romans* (Leicester: IVP, 2001) p116.

[34] R. V. G. Tasker, *2 Corinthians* (London: The Tyndale Press, 1969) p89.

[35] Prime, *2 Corinthians* (Edinburgh: The Banner of Truth Trust, 2000) p44.

[36] Tasker, *ibid*, p83.

[37] John Stott, *Focus on Christ* (Glasgow: Collins, 1979) p125.

[38] Murray Harris, *The Second Epistle to the Corinthians* (Grand Rapids: Eerdmans, 2005) p444.

[39] C. S. Lewis, *The Lion, the Witch and the Wardrobe* (HarperCollins childrens books, 2005).

[40] Mark Dever, *Nine Marks of a Healthy Church* (Wheaton: Crossway books, 2000) p43.

[41] Steve Chalke & Alan Mann, *The Lost Message of Jesus* (Grand Rapids: Zondervan, 2003) p63.

[42] Marshall, *The Epistles of John*, (Grand Rapids: Wm B Eerdmans, 1978) p106.

[43] Os Guinness, *The Gravedigger File: Papers on the Subversion of the Modern Church* (Downers Grove: IVP, 1983) p79.

[44] Martin Lloyd-Jones, *Life in Christ, Vol.4, The love of God* p43.

[45] John Stott, *The Epistles of John* (Leicester: IVP, 1983) p161.

[46] Steve Chalke & Alan Mann, *The Lost Message of Jesus* (Grand Rapids: Zondervan, 2003) p.182.

[47] Chalke, *ibid* p185, 'The fact is that the cross isn't a form of cosmic child abuse – a vengeful Father, punishing his Son for an offence he has not even committed. Understandably, both people inside and outside of the Church have found this twisted version of events morally dubious and a huge barrier to faith. Deeper than that, however, is that such a concept stands in total contradiction to the statement that "God is love." If the cross is a personal act of violence perpetrated by God towards humankind but borne by his Son, then it makes a mockery of Jesus' own teaching to love your enemies and to refuse to repay evil with evil.'

[48] Philip Graham Ryken, *Reformation21.org*, Blog, 1/5/2006.

[49] Stott, *The Epistles of John*, p164.

[50] Dan McCartney, Atonement in James, Peter and Jude, in Hill & James, *The Glory of the Atonement* (Downers Grove: InterVarsity Press, 2004) p181. I am indebted to this article for the breakdown of the categories as they are used here.

[51] Dan McCartney, Atonement in James, Peter and Jude, in Hill & James, *The Glory of the Atonement* (Downers Grove: InterVarsity Press, 2004) p182.

[52] *Ibid*, p182.

[53] Sinclair Ferguson in *The Glory of the Gospel*, 2005 Keswick year book (Milton Keynes: Authentic, 2005) p82.

[54] Alan Stibbs, *So Great Salvation* (Paternoster Press, Exeter, 1970) p42.

[55] Alan Stibbs, *ibid*, p68.

[56] This image comes from Daniel 7 and 12, and Isaiah 29.

[57] Hill, Atonement in the Apocalypse of John in Hill & James, *The Glory of the Cross* (Downers Grove: InterVarsity Press, 2004) p200.

[58] G. K. Beale, *The Book of Revelation* (Grand Rapids: Eerdmans, 1999) p340.

[59] Hendriksen, *More than Conquerors* (Tyndale Press, London 1966) p109.

[60] Justin Martyr *Dialogue with Trypho* p72 http://www.piney.vom/FathJustinDiaTrypho.html.

[61] Hill, *ibid*, p192.

[62] G. K. Beale, *The Book of Revelation* (Grand Rapids: Eerdmans, 1999) p352: 'the present participle – having been slain.

[63] Mounce, T*he Book of Revelation* (Grand Rapids : Eerdmans, 1977) p146.

[64] Charles E. Hill & Frank A. James, *The Glory of the Atonement* (Downers Grove: Inter Varsity Press, 2004) p192.